William M. Anderson
West Shore Commun
3000 N. Stiles R
Scottville, MI 49
231-843-5529
library@westshore

D0936754

Primary Health Care
in Cu'

Primary Health Care in Cuba

The Other Revolution

Linda M. Whiteford and
Laurence G. Branch

With contributions from
Dr. Enrique Beldarraín Chapel

ROWMAN & LITTLEFIELD PUBLISHERS, INC.
Lanham • Boulder • New York • Toronto • Plymouth, UK

ROWMAN & LITTLEFIELD PUBLISHERS, INC.

Published in the United States of America
by Rowman & Littlefield Publishers, Inc.
A wholly owned subsidiary of The Rowman & Littlefield Publishing Group, Inc.
4501 Forbes Boulevard, Suite 200, Lanham, Maryland 20706
www.rowmanlittlefield.com

Estover Road
Plymouth PL6 7PY
United Kingdom

Copyright © 2008 Rowman & Littlefield Publishers, Inc.
First Rowman & Littlefield paperback edition 2009

All rights reserved. No part of this publication may be reproduced,
stored in a retrieval system, or transmitted in any form or by any
means, electronic, mechanical, photocopying, recording, or otherwise,
without the prior permission of the publisher.

British Library Cataloguing in Publication Information Available

Library of Congress Cataloging-in-Publication Data:

Library of Congress Control Number: 2007029759

ISBN: 978-0-7425-6635-4 (pbk. : alk. paper)
eISBN: 978-0-7425-6636-1

Printed in the United States of America

We dedicate this book to the true inspirations for our academic careers—
Marion and Andrew H. Whiteford and Mercedes and J. Howard Branch

Contents

Acknowledgments

As with all books, this one had an evolution. It began in the early 1980s when I was conducting research on primary health care in the Dominican Republic. The similarities and contrasts between the Dominican system and that of its neighbor, Cuba, were both striking and fascinating. Between that time and the initial discussions with Laurence Branch in 2004, many people assisted in the development of my thinking about the Caribbean, Cuba, and primary health care. University of South Florida (USF) anthropology students Dinorah Martinez and Andrea Freidus did research, gave papers with me at conferences, went to Cuba with me to attend meetings and conduct research, and offered a point of view from Cubans transported to the United States. Noah Porter, also a USF anthropology student, provided immeasurable help with the manuscript of the book. Cuban colleagues, like Dr. Enrique Beldarraín Chapel and Dr. Antonio Martinez, invariably provided gracious hospitality and insight into the topics we were jointly interested in. Scholars in the United States like Dr. Lou Pérez, Dr. Helen Safa, Dr. Paul Farmer, and Dr. Arachu Castro shared their visions of Cuba, equity, and medicine with me to my greatest benefit. Drs. Castro and Beldarraín Chapel and I originally discussed ideas for a book such as this in the late 1990s. However, when it became time to write this book, Dr. Castro was unable to contribute because of her other writing commitments, but Dr. Beldarrían Chapel provided the research and the original writing for the initial draft of the sections on poliomyelitis and malaria eradication campaigns. With Beldarrían Chapel's permission, my co-author, Dr. Laurence Branch, and I rewrote and edited that section and we are proud to have it in this book. My immense gratitude and admiration also go to Robert Hackenberg for his astute, direct, and perspicacious comments on an earlier draft of this manuscript. Kind readers like

Karen Wasung Cox, Barbara Rylko-Bauer, Kip Freidus, and Caitlin W. Uzzell helped clarify both the thinking and writing in the book, and their patience is greatly appreciated.

Thus, the book reflects the research and scholarship of many people to whom I am gratefully and forever indebted. My co-author came into the book discussions in 2004, and this product that we are jointly proud of would not have been possible without him. The insights in this volume are shared, as are the omissions and failures. Research support from the Institute for the Study of Latin America and the Caribbean at the University of South Florida made this book possible.

—*Linda M. Whiteford,* University of South Florida

My gratitude goes out to many people who have helped me understand the primary health care system in Cuba. My entrée to Cuba fifteen years ago was through the *Centro Iberoamericano de la Tercera Edad* (Ibero-American Center for the Third Age) or CITED, for which I have been on the board of directors for nearly that long. Dr. Osvaldo Prieto Ramos and Dr. Enrique Vega Garcia, the director and associate director at that time fifteen years ago, have always been generous in their time and support of my efforts. Over these years I have attended a score of conferences and educational activities that CITED has sponsored or co-sponsored. CITED is the premier national tertiary referral clinical center in Cuba as well as the locus for much of the research on aging in Cuba. A referral facility is supported by regional and local facilities. Over the years, I have both studied the primary health care system, and on occasion used it as a patient.

My studies have been facilitated by my good friend and colleague, James T. Sykes, who extended the invitation to attend a professional international conference in Cuba those many years ago. I am indebted to Professor Sykes for opening so many doors for me in Cuba. He has captured many special moments on film, and some of those are offered in this book.

There have been numerous families in Cuba that have taken me under their wing, so to speak, and offered me their insights and understandings about their health care system. My esteemed colleague Andres Amian, whom I met on my second or third trip to Cuba many years ago, shared his language, his culture, his family, and his soul with me.

The family of Roberto, Minerva, Robertico, and Michel in Old Havana welcomed me with open arms years ago and have never let go. The experiences they shared with me were critical in helping me understand the multiple levels of care in Cuba. Their friendship over the years has grown and evolved into a treasure.

The extended families of Santiago, Isis, and Ariel in Cienfuegos introduced me to Cuban life outside of the capital city, and it is a beautiful life. But smaller urban areas the world over have different health care issues than large capital cities, and I am grateful to see through their eyes and learn through their experiences.

Others—Maite' and Lilliam, to name but two—have also helped shape my understanding of Cuba and the Cuban health care system. I have been friends with Maite' for almost as long as I have been friends with Andres. Her lessons were invaluable. And Lilliam, who at one point in her life taught English as a second language in Cuba, helped me understand nuances that my very modest Spanish was unable to deal with.

But my greatest debt of gratitude is to my friend and colleague—and co-author— Linda Whiteford, who asked me to participate in this undertaking. Without her initial invitation, I would not have begun as I did nor finished as we did.

—*Laurence G. Branch*, University of South Florida

1

The Cuban Health Care Revolution

INTRODUCTION

"Nothing in Cuba is as it first appears." The contradictions of Cuba fascinate us, and we are not alone. Cuba has intrigued writers, travelers, researchers, and policymakers for years. In the "Elegiac Carnival," Pico Iyer captures this elusive and yet forceful sense of contradictions: "it is that sunlit sadness that makes it, in the end, the most emotionally involving—and unsettling—place I know; Cuba catches my heart, and then makes me count the cost of that enchantment. Cuba is the old ladies in rocking chairs, on their verandas in the twilight, dabbing their eyes as their grandchildren explain their latest dreams of escape. It is the pretty, laughing kids dancing all night in the boisterous cabarets and then confiding, matter-of-factly, 'Our lives here are like Dante's *Inferno*.' It is the smiles, and open doors and policemen lurking in the corners; and the lazy days on ill-paved streets; and a friend who asks if he might steal my passport" (2004:12).

The Cuban contradictions contextualize the questions raised in this book, questions that describe and analyze the successful Cuban development of an extensive and world-class primary health model within an austere and authoritarian political system. The contradictions are deeply seated in questions of individual liberties and the role of the state; the rights of individuals to be responsible for their health and the role of public health to be responsible for the "health of all"; and the role of the state to reduce inequities and disparities. We believe that the success of Cuba's primary health care model stems in part from Cuba's reduction of social, economic, and demographic inequalities due to gender, ethnicity, age, or region in access to community-based, preventive medicine, a remarkable achievement and laudatory goal.

This book is written so that students, researchers, practitioners, and policy-makers interested in public health can see how one country has put into place an effective public health system based on prevention and primary health care (PHC). Public health researchers have long been concerned both with the Declaration of Alma-Ata in 1978 concretizing PHC and with the many failures to sustain PHC effectively since then (Heggenhougen 1984; Janes 2004; Morgan 1990, 2001; Walsh and Warren 1979; Whiteford 1990). Another concern among public health researchers is the role of equity, both relative and absolute, as a predictor of health outcomes (Wilkerson and Marmot 2003; Wilkerson 1992, 1996). Again, we find there is something to be learned by the Cuban case where reduction of disparities appears to be positively correlated with improvements in health status (Pardo, Márquez, and Rojas Ochoa 2005).

Another point we wish to make in the book is that while we can learn much from the Cuban experience with PHC, we are not suggesting that the Cuban model can simply be picked up and transferred elsewhere. The Cuban model is idiosyncratically Cuban. What makes the model work in Cuba is a response to Cuban culture, history, political organization, and even to the U.S. embargo against Cuba. The takeaway lessons generated from this case are that expensive medical technology is not necessary for effective community-based preventive care, that contradictions within a system are inevitable and can be useful, and that the collaborative roles of the state and the community are necessary to the health of the public.

Cuba, because of its geographic and political isolation, demonstrates the tension between individual and collective rights in high relief. Cubans who disagree with political decisions in Cuba cannot easily leave, and dissent is problematic. At the same time, Cubans have free access to their health care system, and while shortages of medical supplies abound, there is no shortage of medical personnel to provide care. Primary care is available throughout the island; medical personnel are responsible for the health of neighborhoods in which they know and treat the people who live there.

This is possible because individual choices are highly restricted by the government. Movement between jobs, from one neighborhood to another, and from one house to another, is difficult to achieve. But the Cuban health care system has eradicated polio, controlled malaria and dengue, and reduced child and maternal mortality rates to equal or lower than those of much richer and more developed countries like the United States.

This book tries to understand the creation and evolution of what many Cubans and non-Cubans alike call the "Cuban jewel"—its community-based primary health care model—within the larger context of the contradictions so evident in contemporary Cuba. These very contradictions shape the creation of the jewel and include free access to health care for all Cubans, simultaneous with restricted individual rights of movement, employment, and dissent; extreme economic hardships while committing a relatively large percent of its GNP (gross national product) to public health (7 percent in Cuba, 1.27 percent in Costa Rica, and 0.64 percent in Brazil) (Rathjens and Boutwell 2001:2) and exportation of medical care to countries such as Haiti (for child immunization campaigns), Honduras, and Nicaragua (following natural disasters) at the same time as Cuba is further isolated from many of its global trading partners.

To begin to comprehend how these contradictions coexist, we must understand something about Cuban culture and Cuban history, particularly since the 1959 Cuban Revolution. This book is not primarily about Cuban history, nor does it try to compare the current Cuban PHC model with either the conditions in Cuba before the Revolution or with other countries in the Caribbean or the rest of the world. Instead, the book focuses on how the health of one "public" has improved through the process of trial and error that resulted in the Cuban primary health care model at the end of the twentieth century.

The book is organized with the conceptual framework of health equity and critical medical anthropology presented first, followed by a brief introduction to Cuba. Chapter 2 follows the evolution of the Cuban health care system post-1959 as the centerpiece of the Cuban PHC model, family practitioners in communities, emerges. Chapter 3 introduces the Declaration of Alma-Ata on PHC, and how the Cuban national health system has evolved to center around PHC. PHC is a concept about which much has been written and various styles have been conceived: vertical rather than comprehensive care, multilateral financial institutions rather than national governments directing health care policy and practice, and private foundations, like the Bill and Melinda Gates Global Health Fund, funding targeted, disease-specific interventions. In chapters 4 through 6 we pre-sent detailed descriptions and analysis of the four traditional public health foci: child and maternal health, control of communicable and contagious diseases, treatment of chronic diseases, and the care of the elderly. Then in chapter 7 we return to a central question in the discourse on public health: the role of the "public" in public health. The book concludes in chapter 8 with some lessons learned from studying the Cuban PHC example and what it tells us about locating public health as collaboration between the state and the community.

The focus of this book is the development of the Cuban PHC model after the 1959 Cuban Revolution, at which time massive social and political changes were instituted to reduce disparities in living conditions, income, education, employment, and health status. As part of these changes, the pre-revolution Cuban medical and public health systems were dismantled and recreated to better provide equity and access in health care. In the early years, many of these changes focused on delivery of preventive care; much of the attention was on creating an equity-based preventive care system accessible by all Cubans regardless of age, income, ethnicity, or whether they lived in the urban centers or in the rural hinterlands.

According to international organizations such as the United Nations International Children's Emergency Fund (UNICEF) and the Pan American Health Organization (PAHO), by 2005, "the Cuban public health care system easily surpasse[d] those of almost all other developing countries, and in many respects [was] comparable to, or even better than, those of many industrialized countries" (Rathjens and Boutwell 2001). As examples of the contemporary success of the Cuban health care system, Rathjens and Boutwell note that Cuba provides access to health care to 98 percent of its population (surpassing both the levels in the United States and in all of Latin America), and that 95 percent of the Cuban public is attended by doctors and nurses who live and provide services in their local neighborhoods (2001:2). In addition to a high doctor-to-inhabitants ratio (Cuba has one doctor for every 180 inhabitants, compared to 1:480 in the United States and 1:450 in the United Kingdom) (Rathjens and Boutwell 2001:2) facilitating access, medical care is free to all, thereby facilitating equity in access. Rathjens and Boutwell (2001), in nominating Cuba to receive the Gates Award for Global Health in 2001, identify one star of the Cuban health care system—the national immunization programs. Those immunization programs began in the 1960s as the forefront of global efforts to eliminate preventable diseases such as poliomyelitis (1962), diphtheria (1979), measles (1993), and rubella and mumps (1995), while greatly reducing whooping cough, tetanus, and tuberculosis.

The success of Cuban immunization campaigns rooted in the community-based PHC model is deeply embedded with contradictions: Free and competent health care is provided to a population with limited freedoms; effective community participation programs are based on politically-driven community organizations with a variety of other agendas; mass health education is made possible by the absolute control of the market; and labor-intensive medicine-in-the-community operates with few medical supplies.

In this book, we try to explain how this innovative and effective health care model came to be in a context of global isolation, economic hardship, and unrelenting political exclusion from its nearest neighbor, the United States. In addition, we consider the trade-offs required to enable such a health care system to succeed and the very meaning of public health, the role of ideology in its development, and the application of its policies and practices. Rather than provide answers to these questions, our goal is to use the Cuban community-based PHC model to illuminate these contradictions that will pose challenges for public policy and public health researchers and practitioners well into the twenty-first century.

The authors are two social scientists (Linda Whiteford is a medical anthropologist with a masters degree in public health, and Larry Branch has worked in public health for decades) whose interests in Cuba first brought them to Cuba separately in 1992 and who have been visiting and studying the island since. Both authors are scholars whose primary works focus on comparative health systems and public health. A Cuban colleague, Enrique Beldarraín Chapel, who is a physician and medical anthropologist, provided the primary research and initial drafts for the sections on the programs to eradicate malaria and poliomyelitis, rewritten and augmented by the authors and included here with his permission.

Our intent is a book for students, scholars of public health, and international health policymakers who want to know more about the remarkable community-based primary health care model developed in Cuba. We focus primarily on the evolution of Cuba's primary health care model, particularly between 1959 and 2000, and how this model demonstrates that economic strength does not necessarily determine the quality of health care. We selected the years between the Revolution (1959) and 2000 because of the availability of reliable statistics for most of that period. Those forty-one years demonstrate both the unmitigated commitment of the Cuban government to provide health care to the Cuban populace and simultaneously the ongoing evolution of public health policies and practices during these years.

The book is based on our research in Cuba over a period of ten years as well as the contributions from our Cuban colleagues, conferences, and other professional meetings on these subjects. Discussions with Cuban scholars, medical practitioners, ministry officials, and people in the street have deeply enriched our research. In addition to first-hand observations and interviews, a great deal of the material included here is based on statistical data gathered by the Cuban Ministry of Public Health, the United National Population Council, the Pan American Health Organization (PAHO), and the World Health Organization (WHO), as well as from independent researchers.

EVERYTHING IS POLITICAL

"In Cuba, everything is political." This phrase, so often heard in Cuba, also reflects the ways in which Cuba is presented in the English-speaking world. Since the 1959 revolution, Cuba has served as a lightning rod for playing out political disagreements on the world stage, particularly between the island nation and the former Soviet Union and Cuba's neighbor to the north (see photographs 1.1 and 1.2). And those disagreements resonate in many places. For instance, after many years of accepting (and often verifying) Cuban national health data, in 2001, the United Nations Development Program (UNDP) removed Cuba from its Human Development Index

Photograph 1.1.   A billboard near the Havana airport depicting an armed Cuban yelling, "Imperialist gentlemen, we are absolutely not afraid of you at all!" across the water to a caricature of Uncle Sam.

(HDI). The HDI attempts to quantify and rank a country's economic developments, measured by the per capita gross domestic product, with indicators such as health, education, and average income. We do not know why the Cuban data provided to the UNPD were, after years of being accepted, rejected, although Dr. Carmelo Mesa-Lago, an economist from the University of Pittsburgh, recently suggested that Cuba changed its categories for reporting economic indicators about that time (2006). Regardless of the reason, because of the availability of accepted data through 2000, we have chosen to focus most of the book from 1959 until 2000, although in some cases data are presented beyond that date.

CONCEPTUAL FRAMEWORK: HEALTH EQUITY

The framework of health equity that underlies our analysis reflects an emerging area of research, which we combine with the theoretical orientation of Critical Medical Anthropology (CMA). These frameworks assume that, in addition to the obvious biologic and genetic processes upon which Western medicine is based, health outcomes are also the results of less obvious political processes and that politics, powers, and ideology shape provision, access, and equity of care (Laurell and Arellano 1996; Navarro and Shi 2001; Turshen 1999; Morsy 1996; Whiteford 1998b). Access, provision, and in particular equity in health care all reflect political will in the devel-

Photograph 1.2. A billboard near the Havana airport stating, "The most important—our human capital."

opment and maintenance of health policies and practices. Health outcomes, as the Cuban case demonstrates, are influenced by political will and amenable to political interventions that change the social conditions and the social determinants of care (Bambra, Fox, and Scott-Samuel 2005).

For over a quarter century but particularly in the last decade, considerable international concern has focused on health disparities and health equality attributable to demographic, social, and economic characteristics (Doyal and Pennell 1979; Townsend and Davidson 1992; Whitehead 1992; Blane, Brunner, and Wilkerson 1996). One of the reasons for the attention to these two areas is that they reflect divisions within and between societies, social cleavages often based on ethnicity, gender, and/or socio-economic class. Those divisions result in different health statistics for the affected populations, for instance, people living in inner city areas in the United States have significantly poorer health outcomes than do their suburban neighbors; people in rural and remote areas of the United States have more problematic health access than do their urban neighbors, and so on. In contrast to the United States, in Cuba, health disparities are relatively insignificant (De Vos 2005).

One of the great achievements of the Cuban Revolution has been its "other revolution," its revolution in health care. This other revolution resulted in the successful reduction in health disparities and inequalities throughout Cuba between 1959 and 2000. This reduction is particularly visible in the design and practice of primary health care, the focus of this book.

How health disparities are approached is highly political. Some see health differences as the result of individual differences, both genetically/biologically and in terms of economic prowess. Others perceive the same disparities and inequalities as socially created along fault lines of prejudice and stereotypes (Farmer 2004). "Underpinning these different approaches to health inequalities are not only divergent views of what is scientifically or economically possible, but also differing political and ideological opinions about what is desirable" (Bambra et al. 2005:118). Clearly political ideologies shape policies and practices that may or may not focus on the reduction of disparities and inequalities.

In an era when medicine has better information than ever before about the causes and genetic predispositions to ill health, we also believe that "the major determinants of health or ill health are inextricably linked to social and economic context" (Bambra et al. 2005:188; Wilkerson and Marmot 1998; Wilkerson and Marmot 2003; Whiteford and Whiteford 2005a). Many believe that social determinants of health such as housing, education, employment, and income are inextricably linked to health outcomes, yet because access to those resources are governed by policies and practices outside of, and too often unconnected with, the health sector, they are too often left out of plans to reduce health disparities. This isolation of health sector policies from those other major determinants of health creates a disconnection in trying to reduce disparities and inequalities. The Cuban case is an example of how health policy, rather than being an isolated objective of the post-Revolution government, is a central objective and is connected through various other policies and political processes to increase equity and thereby improve health status (Pardo et al. 2005). And the very success of the health sector is dependent upon reducing disparities in those allied social sectors like housing, education, income, and employment.

We believe that the Cuban case provides a carefully documented case of how changes in the social determinants of health are closely associated with significant changes in health outcomes. In addition, the Cuban example demonstrates the power of a consistent health policy and strong political will, even while its practice evolves. Until recently, little data were available that demonstrated how public policy shaped the social environment to improve health outcomes. Wilkerson and Marmot's 1998 publication of this connection drew considerable attention from researchers and policymakers, and their 2003 publication, *Social Determinants of Health: the Solid Facts*, furthered the argument. "Health policy was once thought to be about little more than the provision and funding of medical care; the social determinants of health were discussed only among academics. This is now changing. While medical care can prolong survival and improve prognosis after some serious diseases, more important for the health of the population are the social and economic conditions that make people ill and in need of medical care in the first place. Nevertheless, universal access to medical care is clearly one of the social determinants of health" (Wilkerson and Marmot 2003:7).

Since the Revolution, Cuba succeeded in reducing disparities in income, education, employment, and housing from the inequalities of before (UNPD 1999). Cuba also provided universal access to free medical care, with particular attention on community-based primary care. It reduced the rate of low birth weight babies by increasing care to pregnant and lactating women and to infants, and thereby reduced its neonatal and infant mortality rates to be comparable with those of developed countries. Cuba mounted massive child immunization campaigns and extended life expectancy. "Cuba is the only country to provide protection to its entire population, especially children, against 12 different diseases. Vaccines implemented in Cuba which are rarely implemented in most developing countries include those protecting against hepatitis B, meningitis B and H, and influenza type B" (Rathjens and Boutwell 2001:3). And all this medical attention, including immunizations, is free.

One of the greatest and uncontested successes of the post-Revolution Cuban government is the increased equity in the distribution of health care (Branch et al. 2004; Whiteford and Hill 2005). As Farmer (2004), Wilkerson (1996), and others have made clear, social inequalities correlate with diminished health outcomes. The greater the social inequalities, the less likely the poor are to shield themselves from the social, economic, and health consequences of marginalization and disenfranchisement. Shortly following the Revolution, Cuba identified health as a human right, a right protected by the government and extended to all, thus paving the way to focus attention on the diminution of social, economic, and health disparities (Feinsilver 1993). Regardless of the source of the initial inspiration, health as a human right is clearly deeply embedded in current Cuban health policy. According to Cuban public health expert Rojas Ochoa (2003:161), post-revolutionary Cuba embarked on campaigns to achieve the following public health goals: (1) eradicate corruption in the health sector, (2) give priority to the development of social capital within the populace, (3) plan health policy and implement health programs, (4) develop an epidemiological system of data collection and analysis, (5) create a health system that demonstrates both intersectoral and multidisciplinary integration, (6) search for means of achieving equality, (7) work to achieve and maintain quality, (8) establish community participation in the health system, and (9) achieve a sustainable health system (author's translation).

Underlying these goals is a set of principles that guides the development and ongoing modification of the Cuban health care system. The most significant of these principles is the commitment to free and accessible health care (Rojas Ochoa 2003:161). These principles provide valuable insights into the processes by which Cuba undertook to reduce the social and economic disparities that impoverish the health of a population by exacerbating existing inequalities. What Whitehead and her co-authors (2001) have called "the illness poverty trap" captures how poverty produces ill health that makes it more difficult for poor and sick people to either recover their health or reduce their poverty. The "social inequality/disease trap: a pathological social spiral" is how Nguyen and Peschard (2003:463) succinctly epitomize the effect of inequality on health. Therefore, to improve health, inequality needs to be reduced, and not just *absolute* inequality as was earlier thought, but also *relative* inequality (Wilkerson 1996). That increased equity and a reduction of both absolute and relative inequality improve health is a lesson for global health planners and policymakers.

The Cuban health system gives us some insight into how such an equalizing might occur and is articulated in the following principles (Rojas Ochoa 2003:161) as: (1) health is a human right, (2) medicine is shaped by both state and social forces, (3) health is the responsibility of both the state and the populace—accessibility and free cost for services to promote equity for all of the population, (4) medical practices will be derived from a solid base of scientific applications of the most recent medical advances, (5) the health system will focus on health promotion and disease prevention, (6) community participation is critical to the development and maintenance of health services, and (7) the development of international cooperation in health services will be pursued (authors' translation).

We think these principles are useful not only for Cuba but also could be adapted for use in other countries. The ways in which they might be operationalized would vary, given local country context, but as principles they direct health system planners to improve health outcomes through the reduction of inequities. These principles are distinctive from those that underlie many other health care systems throughout the world wherein health is conceptualized as something to be earned, to be paid for, to be achieved, like a commodity rather than as a human right (Farmer 2004).

The first principle underlying the Cuban health system states that health is a human right for all. That is, it is a positive right, one that does not have to be fought for but one that is a given and protected within the legal system. It is a right of citizenship.

The second principle acknowledges that clinical medicine—its practice, programs, and policies—is shaped by the interests of the state as well as by societal and/or economic pressures. Having a population in good health provides a stronger workforce with fewer days lost to illness and disabilities, and it is in the state's interest and the business's interest to keep a healthy workforce. Social forces as well influence the design and delivery of health care, particularly in a system that encourages, and to a certain degree is dependent upon, strengthening the members of the community through community participation. The second principle, therefore, recognizes that the government has an interest in the health of the population, and also that the desires of the population should have an impact on the healthcare system.

The third principle introduces the concept of equity. Equity is often taken to mean a state, quality, or ideal of being fair, just, and impartial. When applied to health, for instance, it means that health care should not be distributed by some *a priori* rule such as having enough money to buy it or membership in some group or political party, nor should it be provided based on exclusionary rules such as those based on gender, ethnicity, regional preference, religion, or voting record. Rather, equity in health care means that access to health care services should be distributed fairly and impartially. In addition to introducing the concept of equity, the third principle introduces the concept that health is the shared responsibility of *both* the state and the population. Neither has total responsibility for the health status of the whole society; rather, they are yoked together in the effort. Neither can assume the role of the health "victim" as both share the burden and the benefits achieved by good health outcomes.

Quality and science comprise the fourth principle, which states that scientific rigor and first-world quality in health care will be the standards of accountability. As Paul Farmer (2004) and others have pointed out, too often international health advisors suggest to those in poorer countries that they compromise on the quality and/or most recent scientific medicine in order to afford more health care for more people, a supposed trade-off of quality for quantity. That way of thinking blames people for being poor and implies that they do not deserve the same quality of care or the benefits of scientific breakthrough medicine as do those in richer countries that can afford that kind of care. That model often triages health services to provide basic care for the rural areas and tertiary/hospital care for the cities. Given that the poor often reside in the countryside, their care is often inadequate and they have little recourse but to use their scarce resources to gain access to hospital care in the city when necessary. The fourth principle of the Cuban health care system refuses to accept that the poor or those in rural areas should be penalized because of their financial status or their residence in their access to health care.

The fifth and sixth principles are the cornerstones of public health programs worldwide—health promotion and disease prevention and the process of aggressively engaging the populace in its own health care through effective community participation techniques. Health promotion/disease

Photograph 1.3.   A billboard near a large medical facility in Havana stating, "Water that you are not going to drink—don't waste it."

prevention and community participation are two keys critical to effective and equitable health care. Neither is easy to achieve (Heggenhougen 1984; Whiteford 1997). Cuba has a health promotion advantage over some other countries in that billboards, newspapers, television, and radio are government controlled, thereby providing access to health promotion advertisements without having to compete with paid air space as in other countries. Health propaganda is seen on billboards throughout the island. Billboards exhort the populace to save water, wash their hands, breast-feed their babies, and participate in community groups (see photograph 1.3).

However, all too often economists and health planners fall into the trap of conceiving of community participation (principle number six) as either a method to access an inexpensive labor supply or a means to redistribute health responsibility. In actuality, community participation may be expensive, if not in economic capital at least in social capital. To engage members of a community successfully in organizing activities, there must be sustained and mutual trust developed between parties that work for what they perceive as mutually advantageous goals (Whiteford 1997). Social capital is expended when communities participate in government-required local organizing (Whiteford 1998b). The community provides the personnel, and the government provides the training, the technology, and the rationale for the activity. Cuba, for instance, successfully trained local community members to give inoculations so children across Cuba could participate in a country-wide campaign to vaccinate them against preventable childhood diseases like measles and chicken pox. Using the same community participation techniques, Cuba increased its vector surveillance program by training local people in communities to recognize plants that can be hosts to insects like the *aedes egypti* mosquito, the vector in dengue fever (Whiteford 1998b). Neighborhood brigades were charged with environmental surveillance to reduce breeding places for the mosquito. They cleaned up trash, picked up leaves, and removed plants like the dracaena that hold water and provide breeding places for the *aedes egypti* mosquito (Guzman and Khouri 2002; Whiteford and Hill 2005). Effective community participation is expensive because it builds upon and expends symbolic capital, which must continually be replaced, requiring continued and sustained mutuality between the community and the health system (Feinsilver 1989; Putnam 2000; Whiteford 1997).

The seventh and final principle identified by Rojas Ochoa (2003:161) identifies international cooperation in health services. Cuba's approach is multi-pronged. Foreign medical researchers and practitioners are regularly invited to Cuba to attend international conferences, to participate in symposia, and to exchange views with Cuban physicians at research institutes like the Instituto Pedro Kouri (Feinsilver 2002). In addition to collaborating with foreign clinicians and researchers, Cuba exports Cuban health care professionals. In 1998, a letter to the editor of the *New York Times* reported that there were more Cuban doctors than Haitian doctors in rural Haiti (*New York Times* 1998). They are part of Cuba's foreign policy—to provide health care to other countries in need. As Feinsilver notes: "Cuba's development of doctors as an export commodity is unprecedented" (1989:12). Cuba has sent medical technicians, aid workers, and medical brigades to much of Africa and Central America and helped organize significant medical support following the hurricanes, mudslides, and earthquakes in Mexico, Ecuador, El Salvador, Venezuela, and Peru. In each of these cases, the Cuban government paid the salaries of the doctors, technicians, nurses, and other personnel placed in poor countries; rich countries like Iraq and Libya were allowed to pay for medical help from Cuba.

Another aspect of international cooperation in health services that links medical services in Cuba with the wider world is their burgeoning foray into medical tourism (sometimes called "sun and surgery") (Holan and Phillips 1997). People from many countries go to Cuba for elective surgery and relaxation on one of Cuba's beautiful beaches following the surgery. In airports like those in Miami, Santo Domingo in the Dominican Republic, and the Bahamas there are brightly colored invitations to come to Cuba to have one's nose fixed, eyes lifted, breasts enlarged, tummy tucked, and other elective procedures. And then to lie on the beach until the bruises are gone, the stitches healed, and go home tanned, relaxed, and rejuvenated (Holan and Phillips 1997).

Not only are people using Cuban medical resources for elective surgery that they might find in their home country but could not afford, but physicians also are referring patients from all over Central and South America to Cuba for procedures that are not available in their home countries. Weekly charter flights from the Dominican Republic to Cuba carry patients seeking Cuban medical care (Feinsilver 1989:20). Some of the procedures are free to the patient while others are paid for by the patient or his government.

The *Escuela Latinoamericana de Medicina* (Latin American School of Medicine), also known as ELAM, is a final example of Cuban innovative medical international cooperation identified in the seventh principle. ELAM trains students from poor countries, primarily but not exclusively Spanish-speaking countries, as family doctors, free of charge to them or their governments on the condition that they return home to practice medicine in poor communities. Linda Whiteford has visited the facility many times since the mid-1990s and is always impressed by the number of countries in the Americas and in Africa whose students have attended ELAM. Whiteford met several U.S. citizens who were going to school there and who had promised to return to practice in communities in the United States where there were not enough doctors. But most of the ELAM students are from countries like Bolivia, Ecuador, Peru, Nicaragua, El Salvador, and parts of Africa as well.

Attention to the social determinants of health reflects a growing dissatisfaction with the movement away from comprehensive care and toward "targeted" interventions, targeted at specific diseases rather than at underserved or disenfranchised members or subgroups of the society. Since the 1993 World Bank publication *World Development Report: Investing in Health*, the Bank's policy has moved away from investing in governments to help reduce social disparities and improve health, and toward a minimum package of interventions considered inexpensive and effective in reducing the burden of disease. "It should be clear that the minimum package is an attenuated form of primary care, shifting all but a few simple interventions to secondary and tertiary sectors of the health system" (Janes 2004:459). This is significant at a number of levels. The role of the government in providing health care is diminished as the role of the private sector grows, shifting the burden of cost to private insurance systems, social security that is funded by a combination of workers and employers, and toward privatization. Those most at risk are those without coverage either because they are underemployed, unemployed, unemployable, or because their employers do not pay into the system.

Equally disturbing is the attention on the pathologies rather than on their family and individual consequences (Farmer 2004; Janes 2004; Castro and Singer 2004). The reduction of malaria and tuberculosis is important, and they are foci of the targeted interventions, but also important are prevention and remediation for the ever-increasing number of people who suffer from conditions such as heart attack and stroke. "At the heart of the Bank's approach lies a fundamental problem: it is founded on premises that diseases are more important to address than the people who contract and suffer them" (Janes 2004:46). The Cuban case provides an important counter-example to the Bank's current preferred vision of targeted interventions, increased privatization, reduction of the role of government, and increased individual responsibility for health.

A BRIEF HISTORY OF CUBA AND THE 1959 REVOLUTION

One cannot begin to understand Cuba and its contradictions without knowing something about Cuban culture and Cuban history. Cuba comprises 44,200 square miles with a population of eleven million people, many of them living in the capital of Havana (approximately two million; see figure 1.1). Before the Spanish conquest, the island was inhabited by indigenous peoples (Tainos, Siboneys) who died from disease and maltreatment at the hands of the Spaniards who came as early as 1492 and founded colonies shortly thereafter. By 1524, the Siboneys were no longer available in sufficient numbers to provide the labor the Spanish crown required, and Africans were brought to Cuba as slaves. Contemporary Cuban culture reflects the

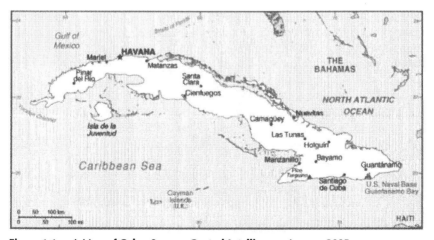

Figure 1.1.   A Map of Cuba. Source: Central Intelligence Agency 2005

confluence of African (heavily Yoruba), Spanish, and other European influences. Both the cultural and genetic inheritances of Spanish, French, and American colonization efforts, along with the traditions, beliefs, and beauty of the African slaves, meld into the Cuba of today.

By 1825, most of the other Spanish colonies in the new world gained their freedom, but Spain refused to give up Cuba until 1898 after Jose Martí, leader of the Cuban independence movement, began the final push to freedom (L. Pérez 1991; Pérez-Stable 1994).

Recent Cuban history, pertinent to our understanding of the 1959 Cuban Revolution and its effect on the current health care system, begins in the 1930s and 1940s when Fulgencio Batista came into power in Cuba. Batista was a sergeant in the Cuban army when he organized a successful revolt by the noncommissioned officers in 1933 and became the president maker of Cuba for the rest of that decade. In 1940 Batista himself ran for the presidency and was elected for one term. Batista ran again in 1952, but seized power three months before the election and suspended the impending election because he was expected to lose it.

U.S. influences on Cuba increased during these times with purported mafia money running into, and being laundered on, the island. In 1953, Fidel Castro, Abel Santamaría, Ernesto Guevara, and others led an attack on the Moncada army barracks in Santiago de Cuba, and while Castro's force was defeated, the resistance had coalesced. Castro was later arrested, jailed, and defended himself in court, making his famous speech, "La historia me absolverá," with which he ended his courtroom defense by saying that it did not matter if the court found him guilty because history would absolve him (Castro 1953).

The attack on the Moncado barracks in 1953 was the beginning of the 26th of July Movement to remove Batista from power and free Cuba from the capitalist system and the influence of the United States. Castro finally succeeded on January 1, 1959, when Batista was forced to flee the country. Along with Batista, the exodus included the vast majority of the country's professionals—among them doctors, engineers, bankers—as well as the owners of large companies. They and their wealth left the island. Since then, many of them have waited eagerly (if not impatiently) to return to power in a post-Castro era.

With victory in 1959, Castro began the process of recreating Cuba in a non-capitalist mode. By April of 1961, Cuba was declared a socialist state and became a supporter and ally of the Soviet Union. Cuba received financial, technical, and military support from the Soviet Union, and in turn, supported it against the United States during the Cold War. The United States imposed an embargo against Cuba in response to the Cuban nationalization of foreign-held industries, many of them belonging to American citizens or Cubans who fled to the United States following the Revolution.

Between 1959 and 1963, Cuba declared itself a socialist state, welcoming support from the Soviet Union, the United States imposed an embargo against the island, the United States broke diplomatic relations with Cuba, and relations finally culminated in the October 1962 missile crisis between the United States and the Soviet Union. The U.S. embargo against trade with Cuba continues, forty-five years later (Pérez 1995).

2

An Overview of the
Cuban Primary Health Care Model
between 1959 and 2000

FROM MUNICIPAL POLYCLINICS TO
THE FAMILY DOCTORS PROGRAM

How do we begin to understand Cuba and its ability to produce a primary health care system that some argue is second to none in its coverage and continuity of care? The Cuban model of primary health care (PHC) depends on both governmental and citizen participation, an extensive network of family medicine practitioners, widespread preventive services, and epidemiological surveillance. There have been significant and continuous improvements in mortality and morbidity rates for the Cuban population, particularly for those living in the rural areas. The most significant improvements occurred in the areas of infant, child, and maternal health, and the control and eradication of some infectious and contagious diseases. To understand how Cuba was able to succeed in increased distribution and access to health care while reducing disease rates, we need to review the evolution of the Cuban PHC model.

The 1959 Revolution, the subsequent Soviet economic support, the U.S. embargo against trade with Cuba, and Castro's longevity and unflagging commitment to public health as a basic human right each separately and together have shaped the development of health policy in Cuba. As Chomsky (2000), Feinsilver (1993), and others have noted, the development of the Cuban health care system was shaped by three assumptions that were central to the Revolution: (1) health was the responsibility of the state, (2) health was a social as well as a biological issue, and (3) health was a national priority, requiring participation from all sectors of the government and civil society. Added to this list, as Chomsky notes, is the fact that Cuba refused to accept the concept that less economically developed countries could not support primary and preventive medicine while simultaneously supporting tertiary or hospital-based care (2000:333). This refusal to concede care allowed Cuba to create a complex health care system comparable to those in the more developed world, rather than relying exclusively on primary care and referring patients to other countries for more advanced care.

To understand how Cuba transformed the health status of the island populace, it is useful to review the history of Cuban policy changes that resulted from Cuban practice-based experiences. The Cuban health experience is intriguing and its paradoxes should serve as lessons. For instance, even with the cumbersome centralized bureaucracy, Cuban health authorities were able to change policies and practices in response to data gathered; initiatives that failed were changed and new programs were experimented with. This approach is significant because it allowed for evidence-based changes, which are both a hallmark of clinical medicine in the United States a couple of decades later and a fundamental principle for Rojas Ochoa (2003). As Cuban health planners like to say, the Cuban PHC model is not borrowed from anywhere else; it evolved through trial and error in Cuba (Castro 2002).

In the following pages we provide a brief overview of some of the policy and practice innovations instituted in Cuba, divided roughly by decades. These changes and their antecedents gave rise to the PHC model in Cuba today. For instance, in 1962, the introduction of municipal polyclinics was an innovation, using multi-specialty clinics as the basic building block for ambulatory care. The polyclinic, staffed by a general practice physician, nurse, OB/GYN, pediatrician, and a social worker (Feinsilver 2002), was charged with providing health care for workplaces, child care centers, homes, and neighborhoods.

These municipal polyclinics become the core of the nascent PHC model. They were charged with providing health screening, vaccination campaigns, blood drives, neighborhood clean-up activities (especially in relation to mosquito-borne disease, since these clean-up activities were actually vector control drives), and organizing community participation through community-based social organizations.

During the initial period from 1962 through 1970, the polyclinics focused on bringing infectious diseases under control through prevention and control activities. By the 1970s, the polyclinics were functioning on a number of fronts by providing comprehensive medical care to all, establishing systems for epidemiological surveillance, particularly as related to vector-borne diseases, providing dental care, and offering postgraduate training settings for medical staff (Novás and Socarrás 1989).

However, the municipal polyclinic model faced limitations. In the early 1970s, an assessment showed that the polyclinic setting was not successful in achieving the goal of integrating medical specializations (Novás and Socarrás 1989). One of the difficulties with the practice was that each medical specialty team worked separately from the others. Their organization and assignment of tasks worked against achieving the goal of integrated medicine and reified the distinctions of the subspecialties. A second limitation identified in the assessment was the physicians' preference for curative rather than preventive programs (Novás and Socarrás 1989).

Other limitations also surfaced in that assessment. Poor community relations among doctors, dentists, and their patients in the community hindered the effectiveness of some polyclinics. Relations between physicians and members of the local communities were often strained. Still another difficulty was that most Cuban physicians were not trained as family medicine practitioners and often had little experience with primary care; they were instead more experienced with polyclinics and hospitals (Novás and Socarrás 1989; Nayeri 1995). As a result of the poor fit between physicians' training and system expectations, both the practitioners and the patients were dissatisfied.

These dissatisfactions led to the modification of the municipal polyclinic model into something called the *community medicine model* (Novás and Socarrás 1989; Greene 2003). In 1974, Cuba tried to improve the quality of care being provided in the polyclinics by adding care for the elderly and treatment of chronic diseases, rather than focusing almost exclusively on the prevention of illnesses. The community medicine approach brought teaching and research activities into the polyclinics, extended the hours to provide continuous care, and instituted assessment and risk evaluations.

However, even with these modifications, the model did not live up to the government's expectations and a reevaluation of the system was set in motion (Novás and Socarrás 1989; Rojas Ochoa 2003).

Notwithstanding the dissatisfactions with the policies and structures between implementation of the community medicine model in 1974 and its later reevaluation, the infant mortality levels decreased considerably between 1975 and 1984 as figure 2.1 shows, suggesting that at least some of the practices of that time were effective.

In 1984, the *family doctor model* was introduced. The new model was based on the findings of an earlier assessment. The assessment showed that both patients and practitioners said that while the community medicine model was an improvement over the previous model, it was criticized because of its unequal quality of care—teaching polyclinics providing better quality care than non-teaching polyclinics. Social factors contributing to health continued to be undervalued, while the biological/technological approaches and interventions for health and illness were considered primary (Novás and Socarrás 1989).

The polyclinic model that came before the family doctor program emphasized technological interventions and biomedical approaches—lifestyle

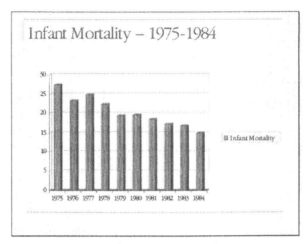

Figure 2.1. Infant Mortality in Cuba from 1975–1984. Adapted from Iatridis 1990.

issues and behavioral medicine were given a low priority, with little attention being paid to family and community life (Iatridis 1990). While these aims and emphases may not appear unusual, as they are common practices in many places, the model did not meet the goals set by the Cuban government. The government wanted vigorous local involvement, significant attention to social factors influencing health, and an overt and articulated focus on improving lifestyle choices for health.

What initially had been seen as an innovative model designed to reach people and provide effective, low-cost medical services was deemed cumbersome, inequitable, and inefficient following the reassessment. The failure to provide an integrated, multi-tiered health care system was exacerbated by the lack of effective communication among the polyclinics, hospitals, laboratories, and other referral services. The relative isolation of physicians from the communities in which they practiced further hindered their ability to participate actively and aggressively in community or family-based prevention programs to achieve health equity (Novás and Socarrás 1989).

These criticisms also may sound familiar to readers with an interest in health policy. Many participants in the health maintenance systems that sprang up in the 1980s and 1990s in the United States and around the world might express similar discontent with their medical services. What is important here is that the Cuban government elicited and assessed information about the services they provided and then tried to modify the model to improve access, equity, and quality. They responded to the expressed dissatisfactions of the Cuban practitioners and patients (Iatridis 1990; Lemkau 2004).

As mentioned earlier in response to the concerns leveled against the community medicine program, the new family doctor program was initiated. It embedded medical facilities in neighborhoods and embedded practitioners in the neighborhood where they practiced, often above the very health post in which they practiced and next door to the families they treated. Having medical practitioners live in the communities where they practiced was an innovation designed to reduce isolation, increase access, improve communication, and enhance equity. This spatial embedding of medical practitioners became a central component of the Cuban PHC model.

The family doctor program continued to improve on many of the initiatives first begun with the polyclinics but also provided greater integration of specializations, improved relations with the community, and encouraged greater community participation. And although the new model was an extension of the earlier model in its aims, the family doctor program of community medicine was also fundamentally different from the polyclinics PHC model (Novás and Socarrás 1989; MacDonald 1999, 2001; Santana 1987).

The family doctor program, as the name implies, put doctor and nurse teams into the communities throughout Cuba. They lived in the community, with the government providing the clinic or health post and above it the apartment where the doctor and his/her family lived. Having housing provided to the medical team presented a significant advantage to those participating because of the ongoing housing shortage in Cuba. In addition to housing and the health post being provided, the program explicitly tied the medical team to the community. They were held responsible for the health outcomes for people in their catchment areas. Perhaps the most fundamental change initiated by the family doctor program was this innovation of the identification of a geographically defined area with approximately 120 to 150 designated families for which the family doctor was responsible (Feinsilver 2002; Whiteford 1998b, 2000; Gilpin 1991; Waitzkin and Britt 1989; Branch et al. 2004). Because residential mobility is restricted in Cuba, the family doctor program personnel would get to know most of the people in their assigned area. Neither the medical personnel nor the neighborhood residents themselves had much geographic mobility, thereby making possible the almost continuous care of families for any treatment not necessitating hospitalization (Waitzkin et al. 1997). Unlike clinics in other parts of the world where targeted audiences are defined by their income, age, or pathology (for instance pediatric practices or infectious disease specialty clinics), the medical team in a family doctor program clinic was assigned to cover the health care needs of a population by their geographic location.

Part of the program's continuous care regimen was attention to ongoing health problems, assessment and risk evaluation, and observing people in their behaviors outside of the clinical setting. Rather than seeing people only when they came into the clinic for treatment as is commonly the case elsewhere, the doctor/nurse team observed people in their quotidian lives. This allowed the medical practitioners to assess behavioral risks as well as medical complaints, to observe lifestyle patterns, and to intercede before conditions required hospitalization (Whiteford 1998a, 1998b, 2000).

The family doctor model of primary health care has intrigued foreign practitioners and health researchers because of its successful emphasis on prevention and community participation (Iatridis 1990; Casal et al. 2002; Whiteford 2000; Barberia, Castro, and Nemser 2002). Its innovations extend beyond just locating the practice and the medical personnel's living quarters within the target community to a focused and active recruitment of the community into health activities. Bringing the community into the practice, like moving the practitioners into the community, has many potentially salubrious affects, not the least of which is enhanced community participation (Greene 2003).

One of the key components of primary health care is, indeed, community participation (Rifkin and Walt 1986; Waitzken et al. 1997; Wayland and Crowder 2002; Showstack, Rothman, and Hasmiller 2004; Morgan 1990, 2001), and one of the key failures of many PHC initiatives is also the community participation component. Medical anthropologists like Heggen-hougen (1993) have argued that community participation in primary health can have a radicalizing effect on the populace. When people come to believe that health is a human right, they are more likely to take political action to achieve equitable health and other services. Certainly such cases exist as in Guatemala in the 1960s and 1970s, when community health workers and others were targeted for death because of their participation in community health/literacy/empowerment campaigns (Melville and Melville 1971).

When community participation is used effectively in social justice movements, it can challenge the status quo and thus potentially endanger the movement's participants. For these reasons and others, governments have been reluctant to provide sufficient and consistent support behind such an empowerment framework. Yet, one of the underlying reasons for incorporating community participation in PHC models is that of "conscientization,"— bringing to peoples' consciousness their power to change their lives (Torres 1993). But Cuba found another way to develop community participation so critical to PHC—by relying on already existing political block groups (Feinsilver 1993; Greene 2003).

Since the 1959 revolution, Cuba has actively encouraged community organizing at multiple levels of the society, from individual blocks of residences to neighborhood brigades to national political groups based on occupation, age, or gender such as the Cuban Women's Federation and Committees for the Defense of the Revolution (CDR) (Dominguez 2002; Crabb 2001; Safa and Federación de Mujeres Cubanas 1989). These political action groups

Photograph 2.1. A young child dressed in her school uniform but appointed with the bandana that symbolizes her involvement with the Cuban civic groups for children watches as a man places his ballot in the voting box in Havana in 1995.

were incorporated into PHC community participation and health promotion activities such as the massive vaccination or vector surveillance programs throughout Cuba in the 1990s (Whiteford and Hill 2005). "They are always watching," people said about the members of the CDR, the block-based political arm of the government whose role was in passing on information and informing community members if they transgressed against the rules or the ideology of the Revolution (Crabb 2001) (see photograph 2.1).

However, in terms of facilitating community-based participation, these extant groups formed an effective basis for enforcing public health regulations. Following an outbreak of dengue fever (a mosquito-borne disease) for instance, members of the CDR actively helped enforce the ban against growing dracaena (a succulent that provides a breeding ground for the mosquito that carried the dengue pathogen). They did so by going into their neighbors' yards to see if they were complying with the new mosquito control ordinance (Whiteford and Hill 2005). One of the many Cuban paradoxes is that this intrusion (and it was considered an intrusion) was possible because of the commitment to the ideals of the Revolution that exalt the role of the state over individual rights (Guillermoprieto 2001, 2004). These neighborhood extensions of the state became the building blocks of the Cuban PHC model.

CUBAN HEALTH CARE SYSTEM SUMMARY

This next section looks at some accomplishments of the Cuban health system since the Revolution such as changes in life expectancy and maternal and infant mortality. Even recognizing that numbers may be used to make political points and that health surveillance and epidemiologic data may be distorted by ideological emphasis, it is difficult to dismiss the remarkable improvement in the health status of the Cuban populace since 1959 (De Vos 2005). This is true even if the Cuban health care system before the Revolution was not as inadequate as has been pronounced by some (Crabb 2001) and in fact, was one of the best in the Caribbean (De Vos 2005). However, no one suggests that the provision of health care was equitable across geography and social categories. Some observers like economist Carmelo Mesa-Lago (2001, 2005) point out that Cuba's remarkable successes in these areas may, in fact, be deleterious to its current economic recoveries. Mesa-Lago suggests that Cuba's continued emphasis on reducing infant and maternal mortality rates following its astounding successes is shortsighted in light of the economic costs that entails.

The following summary is designed to give the reader a brief overview and a glimpse of some of the most significant changes in the Cuban health care system immediately before and following the Revolution:

Pre-Revolution: 1953–1959

- Provision of medical supplies was heavily dependent on imports from other countries; 40,000 pharmaceutical products imported, mostly from the United States (Nayeri 1995).
- Life expectancy was 58.8 years and the number of physicians per 1,000 population was among the highest ranking in Latin America (Alonso, Donate-Armada, and Lago 1994).
- Private sector health care was primarily for the wealthy; the poor had recourse only to the poorly funded and staffed public sector health care.
- Maternal mortality rate was 125.3 per 100,000 live births prior to the Revolution (Nayeri 1995); general mortality rates were also high: 6.4 per 1,000; infant mortality rate of 60 per 1,000 live births (Nayeri 1995).
- Extreme disparities in health care and health outcomes by income; the poor and those living in rural areas were subjected to inadequate sanitation, nutrition, and access to health care (Nayeri 1995).
- Between 1957 and 1967 there were outbreaks of infectious and contagious diseases, epitomized by the polio outbreak that resulted in more than 1,162 being stricken. Few people, especially children, had been immunized, thus allowing for the swift spread of the disease. Since the Revolution, polio has been eradicated and 97 percent of the Cuban children immunized against other infectious and contagious diseases.

First Decade Following the Revolution: 1959–1969

- In the decade following the Revolution, health care was declared a right for all Cubans (1959); the new Ministry of Public Health was created to focus on curative care as well as preventive care to reduce the rate of infectious diseases, resulting in decreased mortality and morbidity rates.
- The government focused resources on improving sanitation and provision of water to all homes (Nayeri 1995).
- Between 1959 and the onset of the U.S. embargo against trading with Cuba in 1961, 75 percent of Cuba's trade was with the United States (Nayeri 1995). The embargo, in combination with the loss of professionals (3,000 doctors, for instance, left Cuba following the Revolution) forced Cuba to search for alternative ways to provide for its population. One response was the development of massive education and training programs to replace the professions depleted through exodus. New medical schools were created to provide physicians in the new health care system focusing on child and maternal health in an attempt to further reduce the levels of morbidity and mortality (Feinsilver 1989, 1993; MacDonald 1985, 1999, 2001).
- The 1961 U.S. trade embargo forbade U.S. companies and their trading partners to send, sell, or provide any food or medical supplies to Cuba.
- Cuba started literacy campaigns, provided free access to education, and the Federation of Cuban Women began health education and vaccinations in rural Cuba (Warman 2001).
- Within six years of the Revolution, two-year nursing education for assistants began as part of the Cuban commitment to improving access to health care. In addition, new laboratories, hospitals, and research facilities were established (Warman 2001).

By 1962 Cuba began a mass immunization campaign to eliminate or reduce rates of infectious and contagious diseases (Mesa-Lago 1998; Beldarraín Chapel n.d.). By 1996, Cuba had successfully conducted thirty-five national polio campaigns and provided more than 64 million doses to the Cuban population (Mesa-Lago 1998). Most remarkable of all is that before the end of the century, Cuba had immunized more than 90 percent of the children and young adults on the island (Mesa-Lago 1998).

Second Decade Following the Revolution: 1970–1979

- In the 1970s the Cuban government consolidated health care resources by restructuring health services to extend their focus to new maternal/infant health care programs and instituted the new polyclinic model.

At the same time, health surveillance and data collection and consolidation efforts began. The following decade saw new municipal polyclinics created and a shift in education policy to training teams in community-centered medicine (Iatridis 1990).

Third Decade Following the Revolution: 1980–1989

- By 1981, "medicine-in-the-community" begins. It is a model of comprehensive delivery, universal coverage, and administrative decentralization to improve efficiency and productivity. During this time, the successful immunization and surveillance campaign results in the announcement of the elimination of diphtheria from Cuba.
- The 1980s saw remarkable improvements in the Cuban health system, culminating in a health care model that focused on: (1) integration of preventive and curative care, (2) polyclinics responsible for total health of specified populations, (3) all levels (primary to tertiary) of services being coordinated, (4) continuity of care by the same staff, (5) follow-up of "high-risk" and chronic patients, (6) specialists practicing within parameters of a health team, and (7) services that included community participation (Santana 1987: 114–16).
- The accomplishments during this period included "100 percent of the rural population receiving health care services" (Iatridis 1990:30) and effective immunization campaigns against polio, tuberculosis, typhoid, and diphtheria to the point that by the mid-1980s they were almost eradicated (Iatridis 1990).
- In celebrating the improvements in Cuba's ability to provide health care professionals in sufficient quantity to cover the island, in 1983, Castro announced that since the Revolution, the Cuban government had trained 16,833 physicians, 4,000 dentists, 30,000 nurses, 29,000 intermediate-level health technicians; built 256 hospitals, 397 polyclinics, 255 medical offices, 146 clinics, 21 blood banks, and 81 maternity homes. And in addition, maternal mortality had been reduced by 50 percent between 1975 and 1984 (see figure 2.2), and life expectancy in Cuba had increased to 73.5 years from 58.8 years before the Revolution (Iatridis 1990).
- People were living longer, children were immunized against common childhood diseases, infant mortality rates were improving, and maternal deaths were decreasing. By any account, these are public health successes. But Cuba continued to reevaluate and revise its health policies to increase the level of integration of local clinics into the national practice system and to shift the emphasis from tertiary and hospital-based care to local clinic care. During this period, attention was shifted away from how to train more medical personnel toward how to in-

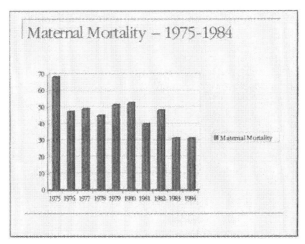

**Figure 2.2.   Maternal Mortality in Cuba from 1975 to 1984.
Adapted from Iatridis 1990.**

creasingly integrate medical practice into the community and to make health a part of community life.

- As infectious diseases were brought under control, the Cuban health profile more closely approximated that of developed countries—increased morbidity and mortality from chronic diseases. The Cuban aphorism—that Cubans live like the poor, but die like the rich—fits the changing health profile as ever increasingly, more Cubans die from heart attacks.

- Unsatisfied with the lack of medical integration and incomplete epidemiological surveillance (particularly of chronic diseases), Cuba again reorganizes the health system into a pyramidal-type administration with local governing bodies created up to provincial and then national legislative assemblies (Santana 1987).

- Simultaneous with the Cuban reorganization of the public health system, their achievements in attaining greater equity and access are recognized by the American Public Health Association (APHA) with its award for achieving "health for all" with universal and free health care coverage (Iatridis 1990). The recognition is well-deserved, as Cuba succeeds in integrating medicine in the community with the "Family Physician" and "medicine-in-the-community" programs, doubling the number of doctors and increasing the number of nurses (Iatridis 1990).

Fourth Decade Following the Revolution: 1990–1999

- The last half of the decade of the 1980s showed stunning successes in Cuban provision of health care to its 11 million inhabitants.

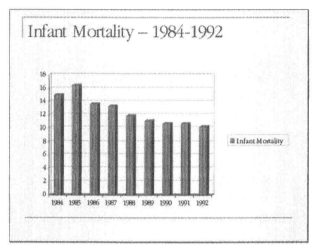

Figure 2.3. Infant Mortality in Cuba from 1984 to 1992. Adapted from Mesa-Lago 1998

- The Fall of the Soviet Bloc—on December 1, 1991, the countries of the Soviet Union declare independence.
- Cuba enters the "The Special Period in Time of Peace" (1990–2004) (Mesa-Lago 2005).
- In 1992, when the Soviet Union disintegrated, Cuba lost its primary trading partner upon whom it depended for more than 85 percent of trade (Nayeri 1995).

Nevertheless Cuba continued improvements in health care even during the "special period" of tremendous deprivation. As figure 2.3 demonstrates, infant mortality shows a continuous decline from 1984 through 1990, even continuing to decline into 1992—during the peak of the "special period." Mass vaccinations continued, covering 90 percent of population against BCG (bacillus calmette-guérin), DPT (diphtheria-pertussis-tetanus), DPT-R, anti-meningococcal B, hepatitis B, and mumps, measles, and rubella (Mesa-Lago 1998). This level of immunization exceeds that of many developed countries.

- Cuba eliminates congenital rubella syndrome while the United States passes the Toricelli Bill (Cuban Democracy Act) preventing U.S. subsidiaries from trading with Cuba and limiting ships from docking in the United States if they have visited Cuba in the past six months (Nayeri 1995). Due to the embargo against trade with Cuba, "Cuba's imports for public health cost an extra $45 million pesos" (Nayeri 1995:326) during a period when Cuba incurs a 4.2 billion peso deficit (up from 1.4 billion in 1989) (Nayeri 1995).

- Cuban responded to the increased constriction of the U.S. blockage and its loss of the Soviet support by asking Cubans to sacrifice more by eating less, using less oil and petroleum products, working harder, and finding alternative ways to do things. The government struggled to maintain health care provision, develop "green medicine" (e.g., revisiting traditional medicinal remedies and growing urban gardens).
- The contradictions continue: After Cuba lost its primary trading partner and the United States tightened the restrictions from the embargo, Cuba eliminated measles and rubella, provided 95 percent of its population with health services, initiated new medical practices, and exported physicians to other developing countries.
- During the special period's most difficult years (1992–1993) and continuing through 2001 (most recent year that reliable data are available), Cuba was 7 percent below the regional average for calorie availability and 13 percent of its total population was undernourished in 1998–2000 (Mesa-Lago 2005:187).
- Again according to Mesa-Lago "Beyond any doubt, on the eve of the crisis the national health system of Cuba had reached the highest levels in Latin America" (2005:189), but continuing to improve these levels became difficult to maintain.
- While some health outcomes declined during the crisis and most improved during the recovery stage, several have not returned to their previous levels (Mesa-Lago 2005).
- The family doctors program personalized and decentralized primary care, but its effectiveness was reduced due to the costs required to maintain it and the lack of availability of most essential medicines by 2001 (Mesa-Lago 2005).

CUBAN DEMOGRAPHICS

We conclude this chapter with a brief summary of some of the primary demographic changes in Cuba that have and will continue to have an influence on the primary health care system and the health of the public.

Figure 2.4 presents age and sex information from the 1999 Cuba National Statistics Office (*La Dirección Nacional de Estadística del Ministerio de Salud Pública de Cuba* 1999). The usual voluntary retirement age in Cuba is sixty years for men and fifty-five years for women, and requires at least twenty-five years of work history. Of the 1.6 million Cubans aged sixty and over in 1999 (14 percent of the total population), 1.1 million were sixty-five and over (10 percent of the total population). With 14 percent of the

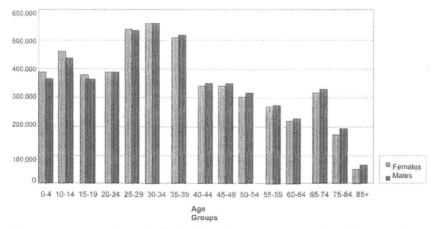

Figure 2.4.   Age and Sex Distribution in Cuba, 1999 Census. Adapted from *La Direc-ción Nacional de Estadística del Ministerio de Salud Pública de Cuba* **1999.**

population eligible for retirement and 10 percent aged sixty-five or older, Cuba's population is similar to most developed countries. Cuba, one of the countries with the oldest population in Latin America, expects that by the year 2025 those eligible for retirement will account for almost 24 percent of the population (United Nations 2002; Mesa-Lago 2005). The increase in the percent of the population retired adds a strain on the smaller percent of the population still working.

Of the urban population in 1999, 14 percent are aged sixty or older, compared to 12 percent of the rural population. Additionally, 13 percent of males and 14 percent of females are sixty and over. In Havana, 16 percent of the population are aged sixty and over. In Havana, 14 percent of males and 18 percent of females are sixty and older (UNDP 2000).

There are other interesting patterns observed in the figure above as well. For example, the fifteen years following the revolution saw a noticeable increase in the birth rates as evidenced by the disproportionately large percentages of the population aged twenty-five through thirty-nine years in 1999 (and therefore born in 1960 through 1974). Another interesting observation is that the population in Havana under age thirty-five is a smaller proportion of the total population in every five-year age grouping compared to Cuba as a whole, while conversely, those aged thirty-five and older in Havana represent a larger proportion of the total in every five-year age grouping without exception. The inference from this latter observation is that Havana has much older residents than the rest of Cuba. Demographers in Cuba suggest that beginning in the late 1980s there was a movement

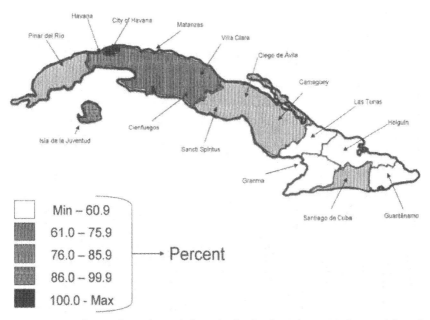

Degree of Urbanization Among the Provinces, 1999

Min – 60.9
61.0 – 75.9
76.0 – 85.9 ——▶ Percent
86.0 – 99.9
100.0 – Max

Figure 2.5. Urban and Rural Population Distribution in Cuba, 1999 Census. Adapted from *La Dirección Nacional de Estadística del Ministerio de Salud Pública de Cuba* 1999.

from the rural communities to the urban areas that continued through the 1990s. Figure 2.5 presents the population density of the fourteen provinces of Cuba in 1999, and figure 2.6 presents changes of the urban-rural mixes for selected years between 1985 and 1999 (*La Dirección Nacional de Estadística del Ministerio de Salud Pública de Cuba* 1999).

Cuba's age distribution in 1999 reveals other interesting patterns. Those under age fifteen comprised 22 percent of the total population, while those eligible to retire (aged sixty and older) constituted 14 percent. The ratio of eligible retirees to children in a population is sometimes used as an indicator of population aging. This index of aging defines the structure of the de pendent segment of the population and tracks changes in the age structure. For Cuba in 1999, the ratio indicated that there were nearly 64 eligible retirees for every 100 children.

Figure 2.7 displays the age distributions for the years 1970, 1981, 1990, 1995, and 1999. While in 1970, Cuba's age segmentation was close to that of a developing country—over 40 percent of the population under age fifteen— by 1999 less than 22 percent were under age fifteen. In 2025 Cuba projects

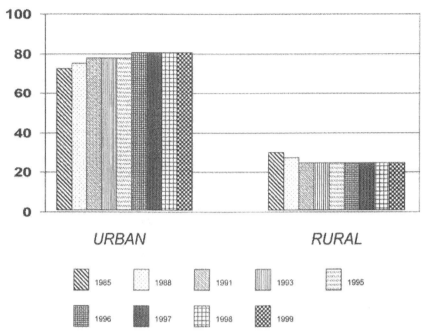

Figure 2.6. Changes in Urban and Rural Population Distribution in Cuba from 1985 through 1999. Adapted from *La Dirección Nacional de Estadística del Ministerio de Salud Pública de Cuba* 1999.

159 eligible retirees for every 100 youths under age fifteen, compared to 122 elders aged sixty and over to 100 youths under age fifteen in the United States (*La Dirección Nacional de Estadística del Ministerio de Salud Pública de Cuba* 1999).

Another measure of population aging that is sometimes used is a country's fertility rate. Fertility rates in Cuba started to fall substantially in the 1960s and 1970s. In 1960 there were 4.07 births per 100 women of child bearing age; there were 3.70 per 100 in 1970; 1.67 per 100 in 1980; 1.83 per 100 in 1990; there were estimated to be 1.90 per 100 in 2000; and there are projected to be 1.85 per 100 in 2010. The fertility rates in Cuba are low when compared with other Latin American and Caribbean countries. Barbados was the only other Latin American/Caribbean country with fertility rates consistently below 2.00 per 100 during 1980–2000. In contrast, six other Latin American/Caribbean countries had fertility rates consistently in the 4 to 6 per 100 range during 1980–2000. In order of highest fertility rates during that interval were Guatemala, Haiti, Nicaragua, Honduras, Bolivia, and Paraguay (United Nations 2002). For Cuba, the decline in birth rates is not only the result of government policy but also may be attributable to ris-

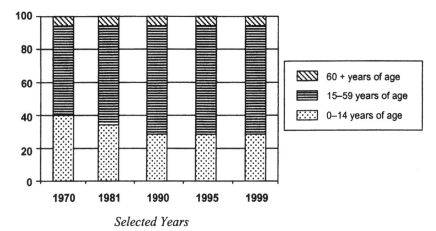

Figure 2.7.   Changes in the Age Structure of the Population in Cuba from 1970–1999. Adapted from *La Dirección Nacional de Estadística del Ministerio de Salud Pública de Cuba* 1999.

ing educational achievements and rising demand for goods and services that in turn encourage women to defer or reject motherhood.

Emigration of young people is also a factor in population aging in Cuba. In contrast to wealthy developed countries that attract young people, developing countries like Cuba often do not. Young potential immigrants may perceive Cuba as an impoverished nation offering few opportunities for jobs and wealth. Cuba has experienced systematic negative balance of migration since the 1960s. Between 1994 and 1998 alone, 150,000 people emigrated from Cuba (*La Dirección Nacional de Estadística del Ministerio de Salud Pública de Cuba* 1999).

In this chapter we have seen how the Cuban health care system—in particular the community-based primary health care practice—has changed through ongoing assessments and evaluations. We have also seen remarkable successes in reducing both infant and maternal mortality, not just initially after the Revolution, but even after those levels were comparable to those found in much richer and more developed countries. Equally significant is that during times of severe economic crisis, the government's commitment to health care delivery continued, albeit without the successes of previous years. In the next chapter we review some of the history of primary health care models, and discuss alternative understandings of the ambiguous and ambitious concept of public health.

3

Alma-Ata and the Concept of Primary Health Care

THE DECLARATION OF ALMA-ATA

In 1978 the World Health Organization (WHO) convened the International Conference on Primary Health Care in Alma-Ata, in what then was the Soviet Union and now is Kazakhstan, to discuss how to improve health outcomes. The resulting "Declaration of Alma-Ata" was approved by that body on September 12, 1978, endorsed by the WHO Executive Board in 1980, and later ratified by the Member States of the World Health Assembly. This declaration, known for its sweeping and broad definition of health and for its commitment to the reduction of health inequities, still stands today as a clarion call for social justice in the provision and distribution of health care (WHO 1978).

In this chapter we review what primary health care (PHC) was meant to be in 1978 and what has happened to the concept since then, with particular attention to how it has developed in Cuba. Few countries have been able to create and maintain a system of PHC as well as Cuba has. To be able to conceptualize what kinds of lessons can be learned from the Cuban experience, we first must understand what PHC is and how it has been implemented in Cuba. In concluding this chapter we return to another document that, like the Declaration of Alma-Ata, has the potential to shape the future of global health policies and practices: The United Nations Millennium Development Goals (UNMDG) (UN Millennium Project 2005). We believe that the Cuban PHC experience offers lessons applicable to achieving the UNMDG.

The Alma-Ata declaration defines the role of primary health care in the following oft-quoted statement: "Governments have a responsibility for the health of their people which can be fulfilled only by the provision of adequate health and social measures. A main social target of governments, international organizations and the whole world community in the coming decades should be the attainment by all peoples of the world by the year 2000 of a level of health that will permit them to lead a socially and economically productive life. Primary health care is the key to attaining this target as part of the development in the spirit of social justice" (World Health Organization 1978:1).

The PHC model emphasizes health promotion and disease prevention, immunization campaigns, reproductive care, and improvements in sanitation and child/maternal health. PHC was also "a model of health care in which human rights, social justice, and equity were central principles. Its effectiveness can be observed in the only national system where it survives today: Cuba" (Janes 2004:459).

As defined in section VI of the Alma-Ata document:

> Primary health care is essential health care based on practical, scientifically sound and socially acceptable methods and technology made universally accessible to individuals in the community through their full participation and at a cost that the community and country can afford to maintain at every stage of their development in the spirit of self-reliance and self-determination. It forms an integral part both of the country's health system, of which it is the central function and main focus, and of the overall social and economic development of the community. It is the first level of contact of individuals, the family and community with the national health system bringing health care as close as possible to where people live and work, and constitutes the first element of a continuing health care process. (WHO 1978:3)

Yet, in the more than twenty-five years since the Declaration was accepted, health disparities across the world are increasing rather than diminishing. For this reason, our investigation of the Cuban system of primary health care and its ability to reduce health disparities is well worth our study.

To be sure, examples of PHC were in existence before the 1978 Declaration and the concept has been adapted in a variety of forms and countries since then, for instance in Mongolia, Mozambique, and Kerala, among others. However, the Declaration of Alma-Ata is useful to review because of the series of underlying principles that are articulated. The following PHC principles from the Declaration of Alma-Ata were identified in a report prepared for the World Health Assembly in May 2004 and are included here to provide a standard set of definitions that we rely on in this book.

According to the 2004 document, PHC should:

1. Reflect and evolve from the economic conditions and sociocultural and political characteristics of the country and its communities and be

based on the application of the relevant results of social, biomedical, and health services research and public health experience;

2. Address the main health problems in the community, providing promotive, preventive, curative, and rehabilitative services accordingly;

3. Involve, in addition to the health sector, all related sectors and aspects of national and community development, in particular agriculture, animal husbandry, food, industry, education, housing, public works, communications and other sectors; and demands the coordinated efforts of all these sectors;

4. Promote maximum community and individual self-reliance and participation in the planning, organization, operation, and control of primary health care, making the fullest use of local, national, and other available resources; and to this end develop through appropriate education the ability of communities to participate;

5. Be sustained by integrated, functional, and mutually supportive referral systems, leading to the progressive improvement of comprehensive health care for all, and giving priority to those most in need;

6. Rely, at local and referral levels, on health workers, including physicians, nurses, midwives, auxiliaries, and community workers as applicable, as well as traditional practitioners as needed, suitably trained socially and technically to work as a health team and to respond to the expressed health needs of the community. (WHO 2004)

These principles make clear that PHC—as intended by the framers in Alma-Ata—is a complex model, departing from the biomedical, physician-driven, insurance-mandated model common in the United States and other countries, distinctive from the governmental, top-down, fee-for-service models common throughout Latin America and different from the dual public/private models common in Europe. The Alma-Ata model requires an ongoing and constant governmental commitment—ideological as well as practical—to health for all of its populace, the education and obligation of the populace to participate in the development and maintenance of the PHC system, and incorporation of primary care as the basic building block of the health system. Implementing such a model requires reinvesting in health as a basic human right and controlling some of the consequences of traditional vested interests in order to "level the playing field" (Whiteford and Manderson 2000).

In many ways, the Declaration of Alma-Ata was a radical set of principles that attempted to change the balance of power in the medical arena—redistributing decision-making and responsibilities between providers and patients, requiring a retraining of the labor force to deemphasize specialty medicine and create more paraprofessionals and family practitioners, and redirecting control to diminish compartmentalization among various health sectors within a system. PHC, as envisioned by the principles laid out in the Declaration, was a direct challenge to existing health care models and was one without a natural constituency. That is, no single group—not policy-makers, practitioners, or any powerful category of patients—is the primary beneficiary of such a model. Each group is required to participate, to uphold a series of obligations, and to meet responsibilities inherent in the model, with successes shared by all.

Key components of the PHC model became the focus of significant criti-cism almost immediately after the publication of the document. Many found the definitions too broad and the goals too idealized. Others worried that the low-cost, labor-intensive model challenged entrenched medical in-terests while simultaneously exposing community health workers to dan-gerous and potentially fatal threats (Heggenhougen 1984; Morgan 1990). Public health professionals worldwide supported the conceptualization of PHC, particularly the role of community participation in health, but dis-agreed with how it should be accomplished (Rifkin and Walt 1986; Walsh and Warren 1979; Warren 1988). Sometimes the distinctions in how PHC is applied are conceptualized as vertical versus horizontal programs or se-lective versus comprehensive approaches to PHC. More often, however, programs are based not on which kind of model might provide the "best fit" with local needs but rather on global politics (Whiteford 1990, 2000) or donor requirements (Justice 1986).

What was imagined as an inexpensive system of integrated, community-based health promotion and provision quickly became expensive to actual-ize. Family medicine professionals and paraprofessionals needed to be ed-ucated, community health workers needed to be trained, local delivery systems needed to be established and maintained, intersectoral collabora-tion and connections among traditionally distinct health sectors needed to be mandated and nurtured, and accepted ways of thinking about health care delivery had to be changed.

In response to those challenges, the PHC model was modified from one that provided integrated care across the population to one that also focused on restricted, vertical programs targeting particular groups such as pregnant women, children, and older people. "Selective" primary care plans were in-stituted that held child health as their primary emphasis. These programs used their resources to develop health promotion materials and distribu-tion systems for a selected number of child health issues: child growth monitoring, the encouragement of breast-feeding, the provision of oral re-hydration therapy for childhood diarrheas, and the provision of immu-nizations.

Without doubt, these interventions saved lives, but they also left many in the community unattended. While PHC models were developed from so-cialist states such as the Soviet Union, the Kerala state in India, China, and

Zimbabwe, by the end of the millennium PHC in its most comprehensive form existed only in Cuba.

THE CUBAN NATIONAL HEALTH SYSTEM

The Cuban health system developed over a period of more than four decades and reflects changing local needs as well as a changing set of international pressures. Following the Revolution, the National Health System (NHS) was integrated during the decade of the 1960s, and rural outreach, primary health, immunizations, and retooling of medical education became significant activities. In 1961 "people's health commissions" were created to encourage increased levels of participation in health care (Feinsilver 2002:A22). During the same period (1965), the polyclinics were established, each having a medical team that included a nurse, a general practitioner, a pediatrician, an OB/GYN, and a social worker (Feinsilver 2002:A23), and by 1974, the medicine-in-the-community program was established.

Distinct from other forms of PHC, and most specifically from Community-Oriented Primary Health Care (COPHC) (Kark and Kark 1983), the Cuban model was dependent on physicians rather than on paraprofessionals to provide most of the care (Mesa-Lago 2005). As a result of this dependency on physicians, Cuba accelerated the production of family doctors and by 2001 had achieved a physician per 10,000 person ratio of 58.2, compared to the United States' ratio of 27.9 and the ratio for the United Kingdom of 16.4 (PAHO 2002). This is even more remarkable when one remembers that many of Cuba's physicians left the island immediately following the Revolution, thus depleting an already limited number of physicians.

During the next two decades, Cuba experimented with a variety of innovative programs, modifying many to maximize their positive effects by consolidating the NHS and ending private medical practice while orienting medical schools to train family practice physicians and developing the national Family Doctor Program (De Vos 2005). By 1975, the concept of "health as a basic right" was written into the Cuban Constitution (Feinsilver 2002). By the end of the century, PHC was well established throughout Cuba, including most rural areas. High percentages of children were immunized, two-thirds of the drugs used were manufactured in Cuba, and doctors were being sent to assist in other countries (Greene 2003; Feinsilver 2002). In 2004 there were more Cuban doctors in rural Haiti than Haitian doctors (*New York Times* 1998).

Cuba was on its way to becoming a "world health power," exporting doctors to other countries as part of its world diplomacy policy and inviting foreigners to take advantage of Cuba's "sun and surgery" health tourism programs (Feinsilver 2002:A24) (see photograph 3.1 for an example of a

Photograph 3.1.   A well-stocked pharmacy for tourists in Havana; one irony is that it is located in a building that has "Johnson and Johnson" across the front arch, suggesting that the building was originally built by the Johnson and Johnson pharmaceutical company before the Cuban Revolution of 1958.

well-stocked pharmacy used by tourists). And finally, these advances led to the creation of the ELAM, the School of Latin American Medicine, to which countries in the Americas (and other, particularly African, countries as well) can send students to train in medicine without cost to either the student or the host country (MEDICC Review Staff 2005; De Vos 2005). According to ELAM's guidelines, once graduated, the medical alumni must return to practice medicine in their own countries. ELAM is the embodiment of a foreign aid practice consistent with the Cuban emphasis on PHC.

Cuba's NHS is organized into three tiers: township, state, and national. The Ministry of Public Health has centralized authority over the Institutes of Health, state health programs, state and regional hospitals, local health departments, and community-based health councils. NHS provides universal free medical attention. Financial constraints such as the loss of the Soviet Union as a trading partner, the U.S. embargo, and crop failures have restricted many medical supplies (U.S. Department of State 2005) and put constraints on traditional curative medicine, but the PHC system still operates (even with few supplies) because of its design, the continued governmental support, the participation of the community, and the presence of the family doctors.

The national health care system is organized to provide health care at three levels (Vega García 2000). The point of entry into the *first level* of the Cuban health system is through the family doctor. The Family Doctor Program began on January 4, 1984 (Labrador and Soberat 2004) and places family physicians along with auxiliary medical personnel (typically nurses) in neighborhoods throughout Cuba. It is this family physician-nurse team, called the Basic Health Team (BHT), that provides primary care at the community level with an emphasis on a continuous patient assessment to monitor and prevent morbidity, mortality, and disability. In addition, an effort is made to assess the social and psychological needs of the individual using an annual "continuous assessment and risk evaluation" (CARE). The family care providers may refer people to other specialists or recommend hospitalization when it is deemed appropriate. Patients themselves, however, may go directly to specialists. The BHT typically sees patients in the first floor ambulatory care setting in the mornings and visits patients in homes or in the hospitals in the afternoons. This health care delivery scheme has made it possible for people in most localities of the country to avail themselves of medical services and care in the immediate proximity of their homes. This is particularly important for those who are disabled or have limitations in their mobility, as is the case of some elders. To be sure, however, the facilities of the BHTs are spartan.

In Cuba, for every fifteen to twenty BHTs, there is a Group Health Team (GHT) organized to support the BHTs once a medical condition has been identified for a patient. Services provided by the GHT are still under the first level of care, even though GHTs are used for in-depth and more holistic treatment (Branch et al. 2004). Each GHT is comprised of a team of nurses and specialists in internal medicine, obstetrics/gynecology, pediatrics, geriatrics, psychiatry, social work, all of whom typically have their offices in a central community or public health building. Two to four GHTs serve a health area where about 20,000 to 40,000 people live. In the case of older adults, a specialized team called the Multidisciplinary Geriatric Team (MGT) serves within the GHTs and is comprised of a family physician, a nurse, a psychiatrist, and a social worker. The MGT uses a comprehensive geriatric assessment protocol developed by the Ministry of Health to promote uniform assessment and responses throughout Cuba. This specialized team also manages the intensity of care that a patient needs and manages those patients in need of hospitalization. Moreover, the MGT coordinates services elders may need for social services and day care centers. In 2001, Cuba had 167 geriatric specialists and 69 geriatric physicians in training.

The *second level* of care provides both secondary and tertiary care. This level of care is comprised of acute care facilities, long-term care facilities such as nursing homes, and other specialty services within the health area. The *third level* provides care for people whose needs require highly specialized treatment developed through scientific investigation (e.g., *Centro Iberoamericano para la Tercera Edad* [Latin American Center for the Third Age]).

The small clinics established through the family doctor program, or *Programa Médico y Enfermera de la Familia (MEF)*, is one of the enduring innovations made possible by the high doctor-to-citizen ratio. These neighborhood clinics, known as *consultorios*, are spread throughout Cuba, giving easy medical access to all Cubans. Each consultorio is located within an identified area (*área de salud*) and is supported not only by the doctor/nurse team but also by the local health brigades. The Cuban Ministry of Health (MINSAP) trained people from the Committees for the Defense of the Revolution (CDRs) and the Federation of Cuban Women (FMC) to work with staff in the polyclinics and consultorios and to assist with health promotion and surveillance. The health brigades (*brigadistas sanitarias*) served to facilitate community participation in health promotion campaigns, reinforce governmental edicts, and exemplify behavioral and lifestyle changes. While the brigadistas played a central role in engaging the community in the health revolution, it was also the continued production of highly trained family doctors that made the depths and level of care possible. The number of family doctors expanded from 10,000 physicians in 1985 to more than 31,000 physicians fifteen years later.

According to Jorge Pérez, the director of the Cuban Institute of Tropical Medicine Pedro Kouri, in 2002 the family doctors in Cuba provided 97 percent of the care (Pérez 2002:A10), with some estimates suggesting that 99 percent of the entire populace receives medical coverage (Barberia, Castro, and Nemser 2002). Also according to Pérez, 74 percent of all outpatient consultations are with family doctors (Pérez 2002:A10).

Primary care doctors in Cuba's PHC model treat families—mothers, children, adolescents, and elders. They provide frontline diagnosis and treatment as well as neighborhood disease surveillance.

There is a broad set of expectations for any physician, but the Family Doctor Program puts physicians in communities for extended periods of time, allowing them to come to know the health needs of the community. When needed, family doctors refer patients to the next level care—the polyclinics that are scattered throughout the country. Nationwide, in 2003 there were 442 polyclinics, and they are particularly important where the family doctor system is not established (Pérez 2002:A11). The secondary and tertiary care systems in Cuba, while not the focus of this book, play a significant role in the Cuban NHS (see figure 3.1). Again according to Pérez (2002), in 2002 there were 281 hospitals throughout the country providing secondary care and eleven specialized institutes providing care in tropical medicine, cardiology, neurology, oncology, endocrinology, and rheumatology.

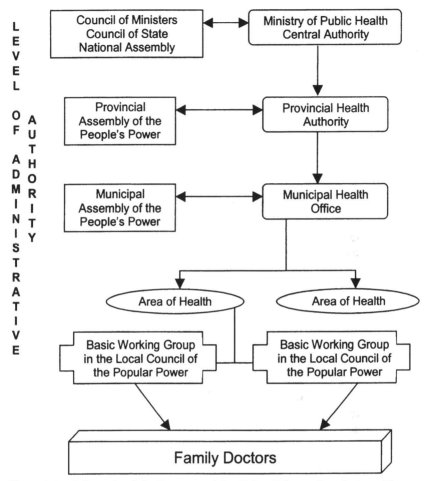

Figure 3.1. Schematic of the Structure of the Cuban Primary Care System. Diagram reprinted with permission from Barberia, Castro, and Nemser 2002

Infrastructure by itself is not enough. What makes PHC in Cuba so unusual is the combination of (1) political support from the top down, (2) continued, sustained, and respected commitment to the idea of "health for all," (3) a medical establishment dedicated to an extensive network of community health clinics and practitioners rather than to specialty practices, and (4) the application of social capital and civil will engendered by attention to health for all, supported by auxiliary forces such as local health committees and reinforced by the CDRs that exist in every community to support the implementation of socialism in Cuba (Whiteford 1996, 1998a, 2000; Feinsilver 2002; Dominguez 2002).

Within the Cuba PHC model, the family doctor program (MEF) epito-
mizes coverage, access, and surveillance. And it also demonstrates a shift
away from a pathology model of disease causation toward a more socio-
culturally lifestyle association between variables such as exercise and diet
and diseases like strokes and heart attacks. As Cuba succeeded in reducing
infant, child, and maternal mortality rates and controlled or eradicated
many preventable diseases, it achieved the early health goals of the Revolution, and the Family Doctor Program was applied to achieving similar goals
with more elusive chronic illnesses.

While aims, goals, and policy descriptions are useful in understanding
what the Cuban PHC is supposed to accomplish, reality often differs considerably from the idealized intentions. Firsthand observations give flesh to
the bones of policy; therefore in the following pages we include descriptions of several primary health clinics we visited in Cuba as examples of
how the system functions in those places.

In 2002 Linda Whiteford traveled to Santa Clara, a city of more than
200,000 people in the Villa Clara province of Cuba, the heart of sugar cane
country. Santa Clara, while not a major metropolis, is nevertheless a city of
significance in both contemporary and historic Cuba. During the revolution, Santa Clara was where the rebels came out of the hills and encountered Batista's troops. The central hotel and other buildings around the
main plaza bear witness to that day with bullet holes in their walls. The
town also hosts schools where children are trained in the fine arts. When
classes let out, the plaza is filled with children, some carrying musical instruments and others carrying their dance clothes. On this occasion, Whiteford visited several small neighborhood clinics where she observed their
practice as well as several social celebrations. One clinic was in an old So-
viet-style apartment complex of tall gray concrete buildings. The clinic was
on the first floor, and the physician and her family lived in an apartment
beside the clinic. Her nurse lived next door, and together they saw the members of the 120 families assigned to that clinic. The clinic was small (four
rooms), clean, and spartan in appearance. Another clinic, covering another
120 families, was set in a neighborhood of small houses spread out over a
number of blocks. In that clinic in 2002, Whiteford met a medical student
from one of the U.S. schools that send their students to Cuba to complete
a rotation in family practice. The American student was observing and
learning from the Cuban family practice physician and was impressed by
what he saw in Cuba: "The skills and dedication of the Cuban practitioners
are inspiring, and I like the closeness they have with their patients. I am
afraid that in the United States most practitioners do not have the luxury of
following their patients and their families even when they are well." What
the American medical student saw as a luxury of time that Cuban physicians have to get to know the people in their practice catchment area is ex-

actly what the Cuban family doctor model was designed to accomplish. The student continued, "Here they get to know them so well; they really know who to treat when they are ill and how to prevent them from becoming ill." When Whiteford asked the young medical student if he thought he would be able to find a practice that would allow him the same "luxury" to get to know his patients that well, he said that would be difficult, given the time constraints American practitioners face, the number of clients they must see, and the mobility of the U.S. population.

The ability of Cuban physicians to be able to "follow their patients and their families even though they [the patients] are well" is a central and significant part of the Cuban PHC system and of its success. In the ideal PHC Alma-Ata model, disease prevention and health promotion are key components to being able to provide low cost services that result in high health dividends. The Cuban political system makes it possible to require that practitioners remain in their assigned community or neighborhood for prolonged periods of time, thus providing an essential element of the PHC system—time. Not only do practitioners know their client families, but also families come to know and trust their resident physicians. The physicians live with their families in the neighborhood. They and their families are exposed to the same problems as the residents/clients/patients and therefore have firsthand experience with whatever shortages, exposures, or other problems are in the neighborhood.

And because they have time, the Cuban family doctors hear stories about what people are doing, what they are worried about, what their concerns are, and whom they are concerned about. Unlike most medical practices in the United States where time is highly limited and practitioners must see as many patients as they can each day, often moving among several offices in different locations and sharing their patient load with four or five other physicians, Cuban family practitioners stay in their single location and treat their one hundred twenty families over an extended period of time. Unlike the United States with its highly mobile population, Cubans have limited geographic mobility, thus providing a stable clinic population (Greene 2003; Whiteford 2000). Limited geographic mobility of the population and limited professional mobility of the providers help make the Cuban PHC model successful.

Medical education is free in Cuba; in exchange, physicians complete their rural internships and establish their practice where the government assigns them—often in the neediest of areas. Physicians earn the equivalent of between $30 and $40 a month and for many years were not allowed to take second jobs. They were expected to be physicians and only physicians (Lemkau 2004). In addition, the state provides them with education, health care, utilities, and housing—often in scarce supply—for themselves and their families. Physicians are sometimes provided a vehicle to see patients,

Photograph 3.2.   Inside the office of a Basic Health Team in a neighborhood of Havana in 2001; there is a reusable metal syringe soaking in tap water in a metal sputum in the porcelain sink, next to metal basin for cleansing medical instruments, that in turn is next to an autoclave used to kill bacteria.

with ration coupons for fuel. Like their neighbors, physicians rely on ration coupons for food that is never in abundance, and what is available is shared. It is not a life of abundance, but it is one of being needed and responding to that need. As one Cuban told a researcher: "We are a country of shared poverty, but not shared misery" (Lemkau 2004).

The clinic observed in Santa Clara shared many similarities with the clinics that Branch visited in Havana in 1998. Like the clinics in Santa Clara, the Havana clinic had four rooms on the first floor of the building, while the physician and her family lived on the second floor. While clean, the clinic's materials were not new: Branch noticed a pitted porcelain sputum containing two glass and steel hypodermic needles sitting in water (not alcohol) awaiting reuse beside the sink that showed rust stains of many years (see photograph 3.2 that was taken in 1997).

At that time, Branch did not see any computers in clinics; instead, an extensive hardcopy patient filing system was being used by the physician-nurse pair. The clinic personnel were proud that their patient records allowed them continuity and facilitated timely care for their patients. Even without computers, Branch saw no lack of preparedness among the numerous providers, all of which serves to remind that computer-assisted patient record systems are a means of coordinating comprehensive care, but coordinated comprehensive care can be achieved without computers.

When Branch visited another clinic in the capital, he observed a visiting physician from Canada who was impressed by the health promotion and disease prevention efforts of the family practice clinics. The Canadian physician asked the Cuban doctor how many of his patients had hypertension, and the family doctor replied that about 30 percent of them did. The Canadian physician then asked what percentage of those patients were on medication for their hypertension. The Cuban doctor's response was that almost none of them were on medication. The answer seemed to surprise the Canadian physician, but his concern was quickly replaced by admiration when he learned that Cuban family doctors are very serious about controlling hypertension through diet and exercise. In their system with scarce medical supplies, Cuban physicians expect their patients to be compliant with proscriptions of diet and exercise, and only use medications in rare circumstances.

As we have learned, in Cuba things are not always as they first appear. What at first appeared to be a clinic without necessary record-keeping equipment (computers) or sufficient medications, upon more careful analysis was a clinic with adequate record keeping and a reliance on controlling hypertension through behavior change: diet and exercise.

One of the advantages of the Cuban Family Doctor model of PHC is that in addition to the traditionally targeted areas of disease prevention and health promotion, particularly for maternal and child health, the community doctor model recognizes the double burden that many countries experience when they successfully reduce early mortality, resulting in increased chronic diseases (Kekki 2003; Janes 2004). Many developing countries today struggle to reduce maternal and child mortality due to infectious disease, and they subsequently face increased levels of chronic diseases that place new burdens on health care providers and families. In those countries that succeed in these aims, the population pyramid changes: More people than ever before in poor and developing countries are living longer, often suffering from the same chronic and debilitating diseases that beset richer, more developed countries. As a larger number of the population lives longer, countries face new health care obstacles.

In Cuba, where the number of elderly people has continued to increase as life expectancy has been extended through better health care, family doctors have access to *Circulos de Ancianos* (Reunions of Elders) where elderly people gather while their family members are at work during the day. Many centers provide company, a meal, and day care for elderly dementia patients (see photograph 3.3). Elders in Cuba have access to resources targeted specifically for people of *la tercera edad* (the third age) providing them with organized activities, exercise, communal tasks, and health care

Photograph 3.3.   The back courtyard of a community senior center in 2001; the seniors are participating in facilitator-led exercises, however it is interesting to note that the seniors had to walk down a steeply inclined paved driveway to reach the courtyard.

(see chapter 6 for a more detailed discussion). Family doctors work closely with their communities, often noticing changes in elders before family members do and are able to work together with them to find locally available solutions. Close attention to local needs allows resources to be relatively equitably distributed. While the Cuban PHC model emphasizes preventive care and health promotion, particularly among the younger segments of the population, diseases associated with long life are also, and increasingly, addressed.

The Declaration of Alma-Ata identified "equity" as a component in the "health for all" ideal. Again, according to Janes, equity in distribution of health care can be measured using three variables: "(1) fair mobilization of resources to pay for health care (termed 'vertical' equity); (2) needs-based distribution of health services—in terms of access, quality, and type of care ('horizontal' equity); and (3) fair protection afforded to individuals and families from the consequences of catastrophic illness" (2004:461). He also adds, citing international health policy researchers (Kawabata, Kei, and Carrin 2002; Narayan et al. 2000; Wagstaff 2002; Sachs and the Commission on Macroeconomics and Health 2001), that the three criteria identified above mirror WHO objectives for *any* health care system.

THE WHO COMMISSION ON
MACROECONOMICS AND HEALTH

Chaired by Dr. Jeffry Sachs, the WHO Commission on Macroeconomics and Health released its report in December 2001 (WHO 2001). That report may well shape global health policy for decades into the new millennium. Like the 1993 *World Bank Report on Health and Development*, the WHO Commission on Macroeconomics and Health is already having both immediate and long-term effects on decision making about development and health services (Kekki 2003). One of the most significant effects of this document is the continued "economization" of health; reconceptualizing health not as a human right but as a component of economic development. In such a schema, the ability to measure program outcomes is in terms of some definition of efficacy, which becomes more important than the reduction of human suffering and ill health.

The WHO Commission on Macroeconomics and Health made ten recommendations relevant to our discussion of PHC. These ten recommendations remind us that in all systems some trade-offs are necessary. In that report, the authors recommended the following: (1) an increase in universal access to health services; (2) establishment of National Commissions on Macroeconomics and Health; (3) an increase in donor country financial support and investment in health; (4) that WHO and the World Bank increase and coordinate their support for "scaling-up" and monitoring activities; (5) that the World Trade Organization (WTO) allow poor countries relief from compulsory licensing from third country generic suppliers; (6) a strengthening of international health agencies; (7) bolstering of the supply of global public goods by financing agencies such as the World Bank; (8) an increase in private-sector incentives for drug development for diseases common among the poor, such as TB and malaria; (9) that essential medicines should be produced at low costs and distributed equitably in low-income countries by the international pharmaceutical industry; and (10) that the International Monetary Fund (IMF) and the World Bank work with recipient countries to incorporate scaling up of health and other poverty-reduction programs into viable economic frameworks (Kekki 2003:5). According to the authors of the Commission report, if essential interventions were scaled up worldwide, eight million lives could be saved each year by 2010 (Sachs and the Commission on Macroeconomics and Health 2001).

Even though there are many variants of the Alma-Ata PHC model, the basic principles remain: essential health care; universal access; commitment, participation, and community self-reliance; intersectoral action; cost-effective and appropriate technology; and health service provision and health promotion. What is of interest to us here is how those goals were achieved in the

Cuban case and what kinds of trade-offs were necessary in order to achieve those goals. Could such goals be achieved in a free choice system or are they only possible to achieve in a limited choice system such as in Cuba? We concur with Pertti Kekki who wrote the Executive Summary for the WHO report on primary health care and the Millennium Development Goals (2003). He noted four trends: the current trends in diseases, particularly the increased levels of non-infectious disease; the demographic trends of increased proportions of the elderly compared to midlife members of a country; the social trends in globalization, urbanization, and industrialization; and the trends toward increased poverty and overall inequalities. In light of these trends, we have an obligation to seek reconciliation between the disparate health care models and understandings of rights/responsibilities in providing health to the public.

In the next chapters we look at the Cuban PHC model in terms of the classic public health categories: child/maternal health (chapter 4); infectious and communicable diseases (chapter 5); and chronic diseases and the elderly (chapter 6).

4

The Cuban Primary Health Care Model for Child and Maternal Care

"It's excessive; if the baby and the mother are both well they don't need to be seen that often." That was the response of an American doctor when a Cuban family practice physician told him how often Cuban newborn babies and their mothers were seen in the first six months after birth. Then the American doctor asked, "Your clinic must be full all the time with mothers and their well babies. How do you have time for anything else?" In 1993 when this discussion took place in a neighborhood clinic in Matanzas, few North Americans knew much about the Cuban health care system and even less about the medicine-in-the-community campaign that took health care practice into neighborhoods. The American doctor was taken aback by the response from the Cuban doctor when he said, "They don't come into the clinic. I go see them in their homes. While I am there I see the baby and mother, but I also see the grandmother, the elderly uncle, and the teenage daughter. I can see how they are feeling; I can see if the grandmother is depressed, if the daughter needs someone to talk to about birth control, if the uncle is drinking too much. And I can see how they are responding to the new baby. And because I go so often I can see if there are changes in the family over time. No, it's not excessive if I can see five or six people and help forestall problems that might deteriorate without some attention."

We left impressed. Suddenly the use of the physician's time in well-baby visits that were also family-based prevention did not seem excessive but rather an efficient use of time and training where the ratio of physician to population is higher than most other places in the world—including the United States (Iatridis 1990:30). In Cuba, healthy babies under one year old have fifteen required doctor visits; children between one and four years old are seen twelve times a year, and children between five and fourteen years

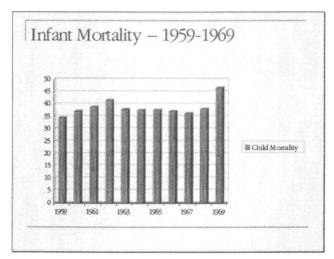

Figure 4.1.   Infant Mortality in Cuba from 1959–1969. Adapted from Iatridis 1990.

old are seen about eleven times a year (Donate-Armada 1994). That makes about thirty-eight required doctor visits for Cuban children between the ages of one and fourteen, compared with the twenty-two visits for American children from prenatal to twenty years old (Donate-Armada 1994).

According to WHO and other global health organizations, health care for all strategies must be concerned with both medical outcomes and social impacts (Iatridis 1990). The medical outcomes most often used to assess health of a nation are maternal and infant mortality, child mortality, life expectancy, and mortality due to infectious and chronic diseases. These measures, in combination with the revolutionary idea that physicians are responsible for all those people living in a geographic area rather than just a number of patients, contributed to the success of the medicine-in-the-community model.

Figures 4.1 and 4.2 show levels of infant and maternal mortality in the decade following the Revolution. Infant mortality remained relatively unchanged during that period of time, with a slight increase immediately after the Revolution. Since infant mortality reflects prenatal care and nutrition as well as conditions during and immediately following birth, it is not unusual to see such a pattern as a reflection of social upheaval. Maternal mortality showed a decreasing trend over this interval. Maternal mortality more often reflects conditions of labor and delivery as well as prenatal care attention.

During the latter half of the first decade after the Revolution, maternal mortality began to decline, reflecting improvements in prenatal attention and in labor and delivery conditions. In the years that follow and as the PHC

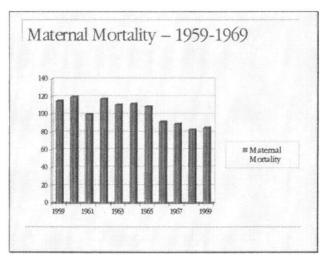

Figure 4.2. Maternal Mortality in Cuba from 1959–1969. Adapted from Iatridis 1990.

programs evolved, pregnant women were seen both in their homes and in the neighborhood clinics during their pregnancies and following the birth of the children. By 1995 the standard number of prenatal visits was about twelve. Pregnant women were given coupons to receive extra rations of scarce foods needed for the developing fetus. Over time, particularly during the "special period," ration coupons too often did not cover the woman's nutritional needs, and even if they did, food was difficult to find (Mesa-Lago 2005). During both pregnancy and lactation, women's bodies require considerably more folic acid, protein, and dairy products. The times during which the government provides extra rations reflect the government's concern with prenatal development and with women's health. That concern, some argue, becomes translated into coercion, with members of CDR acting as enforcers rather than supporters (Crabb 2001; Alonso et al. 1994).

Pregnant women are required to be seen by their neighborhood doctors. If a woman fails to make an appointment, she is often visited by members of the CDR in her neighborhood. Women are tested for genetic abnormalities and women with hypertension or diabetes are often counseled to consider the possibility of abortion (Donate-Armada 1994). The very real specter of government coercion to improve health outcomes raises age-old questions about how to achieve public health, especially when an individual within the community may not be particularly willing to comply with measures deemed necessary by medical and/or governmental authorities. In the early 1980s, failure of the U.S. public to inoculate children against infectious/contagious childhood diseases resulted in legislation requiring immunizations before students were allowed to enroll in public schools. In the U.S. case, the government decided against individual rights to choose whether to inoculate, and the government enforced inoculations in order to protect the public from preventable infectious childhood diseases. In 2004, even college-age students in the United States were required to demonstrate inoculation records or delay entrance to university until they were immunized. Some argue that this is coercion; others say it is simply protecting the public's health by reducing the risk of preventable epidemics. But these cases raise questions about the appropriate role of the state in challenging individual rights for the "greater good" of an amorphous public. These same concerns were raised again by Cuba's policies pertaining to the control of HIV/AIDS (Burr 1997; Iatridis 1990; MacDonald 2001; Parameswaran 2004; Scheper-Hughes 1993).

The questions raised by the discussion of how to balance individual rights with the rights of the state as they apply to public health concerns are not small questions. What should the state be allowed to force their citizens to do in the name of "public safety"? Two of the most significant recent public health documents—the Declaration of Alma-Ata and the Millennium documents—stress health-for-all, but not how to balance governmental strategies to achieve the desired health outcomes with the populace's need for autonomy and independence.

Whether through national policies and/or coercive practices, the Cuban medicine-in-the-community initiative succeeded in instituting a program locating family practitioner teams in specific neighborhoods to care for identified populations and develop health promotion campaigns that resulted in enviable levels of child and maternal mortality in Cuba. Many in the more developed world live with health disparities based on education, ethnicity, and income that result in barriers to access that far exceed the barriers found in Cuba. The oft-repeated statistic that the infant mortality in Cuba was 6.2 per 100,000 live births in 2000, compared to a rate of 7.2 in the United States, underscores this point (PAHO 2005).

Without doubt, epidemiological results are politicized (Crabb 2001). Governments use numbers to support their programs, policies, arguments, and ideologies. In addition to numbers being used politically, the accuracy of numerical reports varies depending on source, years analyzed, and integers used, let alone who is doing the reporting, for whom, and how the information is gathered and stored. In most countries, diagnostic categories change when a critical mass of data and/or social pressure change. For instance, the Diagnostic and Statistical Manual (DSM) that is widely accepted to provide categories of diagnosis and their symptoms changes every so often. Currently practitioners are working with the DSM-IV-TR, which means the DSM has been revised four times and the last revision had text revisions. The very process of revising worldwide standards of diagnoses means that the number of cases of a particular diagnosis may change significantly, not because there are more or fewer people experiencing those symptoms but only that the way the information is gathered, categorized, stored, or retrieved has changed. For that reason, it is valuable to use multiple sources of information when looking at health statistics, particularly where computerized data collection, storage, and retrieval are neither universally nor historically experienced. The economist Dr. Carmelo Mesa-Lago mentions that in 2001 Cuba changed a number of year-based calculations for internal macroeconomic indicators (Mesa-Lago 2005) that makes some macroeconomic calculations following that year problematic.

However, by any count, levels of infant, child, and maternal mortality have decreased significantly since the 1959 Revolution in Cuba (see figures 4.3–4.6). This continual, if not constant, decrease in mortality rates among women, infants, and children is remarkable given that these decreases were not found across-the-board in other countries of Latin America and the Caribbean. In addition, these decreases continued under conditions of scarcity, political stress, and great economic uncertainty. Even during the "special period" mortality rates continued to decline, although there were some spikes in infant and maternal mortality following the loss of Cuba's

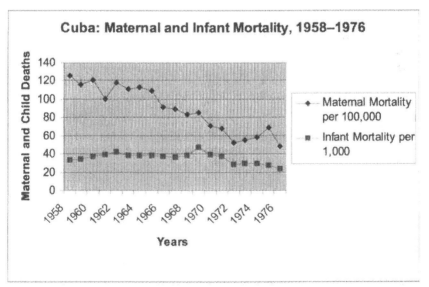

Figure 4.3. Maternal and Infant Mortality in Cuba, 1958–1976. Adapted from PAHO 2004.

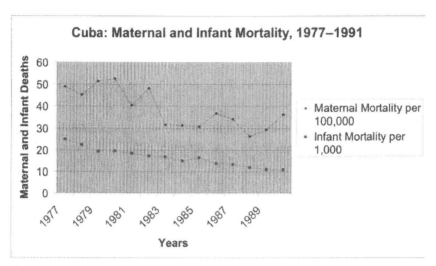

Figure 4.4. Maternal and Infant Mortality in Cuba, 1977–1991. Adapted from PAHO 2004.

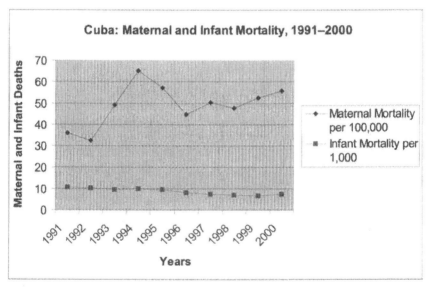

Figure 4.5. Maternal and Infant Mortality in Cuba, 1991–2000. Adapted from PAHO 2004.

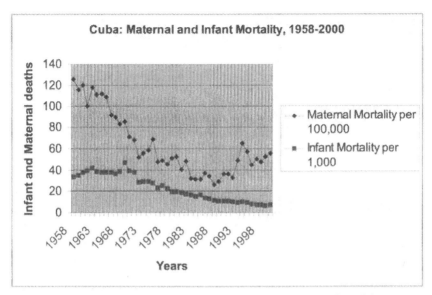

Figure 4.6.   Maternal and Infant Mortality in Cuba, 1958–2000. Adapted from PAHO 2004.

primary trading partner, the former Soviet Union. Even as late as 2001, infant mortality rates continued to decline, a difficult task when they were already low. While infant mortality declined, the early part of the new millennium showed some small increases in maternal mortality (Mesa-Lago 2006).

Public health professionals recognize that changing health outcomes from "very bad" to "better" can be accomplished through the provision of potable water and sanitation, access to medical care, and effective immunization campaigns. This means that radical and significant infrastructure changes can result in true changes in basic health outcomes. Clean water reduces the number of infants and children that die needlessly from preventable diarrheas. Sanitary systems mean that fewer infants, children, and other vulnerable populations die from infectious oral-fecal diseases like cholera. Provision of accessible and reliable medical services, immunization campaigns, and prenatal care mean that fewer children, pregnant or lactating women, and elderly die from preventable illnesses. Between 1959 and 2000, Cuba successfully accomplished all of this. Most public health professionals also realize that changing health outcomes from "pretty good" to "good" is immensely difficult. And, as the data leading up to 2000 demonstrate, Cuba did that as well (see photograph 4.1).

Once there are clean water, sanitary systems, accessible and affordable health care, routine medical access, and immunizations, why does the level

Photograph 4.1.   With the improving health outcomes come improving qualities of life; for these three children their quality of life is expressed in the breadth of their smiles.

of infant, child, and maternal mortality continue to decrease? In many countries, the mortality rates level off once public health has achieved clean water, health access, and sewerage. But in Cuba, the rates continued to decrease, even in the prolonged "special period" of economic hardship and scarcity. This continual improvement may, in fact, be partially accounted for by the continual policy and program revisions within the Ministry of Public Health (MINSAP). We have also seen ample evidence, both statistical and observational, that the continual improvement in Cuba's infant, child, and maternal health indicators also reflects the role played by local community health participation and promotion activities as well as by the government and neighborhood health brigades.

Health promotion is defined as "all those activities that are intended to prevent disease or to promote positive health" (Kemm and Close 1995:25), not unlike the statement from the 1978 Alma-Ata Resolution: "The main social targets of governments and of the World Health Organization (WHO) in the coming decades should be the attainment by all citizens of the world by the year 2000 of a level of health that will permit them to lead a socially and economically productive life" (Donaldson and Donaldson 1994:118). According to Greene, health promotion as a recognized field focuses on the nexus between governmental and private individual activities and initially was derived from three documents: the Lalonde Report in

1974, the WHO Global Strategy in 1981, and the Ottawa Chapter in 1986 (2003:107).

The three reports converged on the view of health as a resource that needed, even demanded, government interventions. According to Bennett (1999:32): "Health promotion policy encompasses diverse, but complimentary approaches to improving health, including legislation, taxation and organization and environmental change as inequities arise, at least in part, from social educational disadvantage." Therefore, at least according to this view of health promotion, governments must work with individuals to change individual and community lifestyles and improve their health status so that they can live longer and without disabilities. It is not surprising that government interventions could be construed not only as acceptable but also as necessary. After all, the development and maintenance of a productive labor force is critical to economic productivity. Days lost to illness are a loss not only to individuals and families but also to communities and labor.

In the United States there was a similar move of passive and then more active government intervention when the government, through the Office of the United States Surgeon General, first issued warnings on the association of cigarette smoking and health in 1964 (Smoking and Health 1964). At first there were warnings, then a ban on showing smoking in certain types of the media, and more recently both a federal ban on smoking in some workplaces and restaurants and increased costs of insurance policies for those who smoke. Lifestyle changes—whether smoking cessation or exercise regimens—do not come easily. The U.S. experience shows, as Donaldson and Donaldson (1994:81) suggest, how health promotion needs to encompass a multi-pronged strategy that "embraces a wide variety of perspectives from preventing premature death to legislative and fiscal measures to improve health, the promotion of individual responsibility for the maintenance of health, ways of living and to mobilize support of communities as part of health improvement programmes."

Having moved forward in the post-revolutionary era in the education of more physicians, the production of more clinics, the increase in population literacy, and a reduction of levels of mortality and morbidity, by 1974, Cuba began focusing on health promotion strategies. As in other countries, attention began to focus on ways to influence lifestyle changes and thereby improve health status outcomes. For instance, by 1975, health promotion in Canada was still being discussed as a philosophical issue but by that time "in Cuba it was happening" (MacDonald 2001:228–229). In the United States and other countries, health promotion campaigns are often instigated by large companies whose products are marketed to help people get healthy rather than responding to an identified need to increase social awareness. Smoking cessation campaigns in the United States, for instance, are often underwritten by products purchased for that purpose (i.e., stop-smoking products).

But because Cuba had limited private enterprise, the government is the primary instigator and facilitator of health campaigns. Often the health promotion message is plastered on billboards (see photograph 1.3 on page 12) with nationalistic slogans like "Conserve Water for the Revolution" or "Our Children Are the Future of the Revolution: Protect Their Health." Cuba's health promotion policies from the 1970s were not based on clinical interventions but rather on developing broad social awareness of the variables that link lifestyles, personal habits, and health. MacDonald writes that health promotion in Cuba is based on "personal autonomy and high self-esteem leading to neighborhood advocacy and ultimately to inter-sectoral collaboration" (2001:229).

We, however, believe that much of the efficacy of Cuban health promotion lies in the organization of neighborhood brigades designed initially to defend Cuba from foreign aggressors but which have evolved into many other activities. These "revolutionary brigades," like the CDRs (Committees for the Defense of the Revolution), function to keep neighborhoods as units, coordinate the dispersal of goods, keep track of their neighbors' activities (i.e., are they renting out a room to a foreigner without a license [Crabb 2001]), and surveillance that patios are clear of dracaenas (Whiteford 1997)). Young Pioneers (YP), the brigade of school-age children in the national political party, participate in parades, perform at school functions, and are asked to entertain foreign visitors in public receptions. The neighborhood brigades are encouraged to recruit children to participate in the YP and put pressure on parents whose children do not participate (Crabb 2001). YPs and neighborhood brigades channel information from the government through clinics, schools, and direct contact with government agencies about activities in which neighborhood members are expected to participate. Following an outbreak of dengue fever, local neighborhood brigades combed family gardens and little yards to ferret out plants that hold water and could become potential breeding sites for the dengue-fever vector after a government edict outlawed the plants (Whiteford and Hill 2005).

Whether one views the neighborhood brigades as overly coercive or simply facilitative, the brigades unquestionably promulgate the government's health promotion activities. While they are but one way in which Cuba's health promotion activities occur, the brigades are effective, and their role in transmitting the government's desire for good health outcomes is undeniable.

5

The Cuban Experience with Controlling Infectious and Communicable Diseases through Primary Health Care

Before as well as immediately after the 1959 revolution, Cuba faced high mortality rates specifically from communicable diseases that affected young and old, males and females alike. The domestic mortality picture was typical of underdeveloped nations where infectious diseases such as malaria, poliomyelitis, diphtheria, typhoid fever, tuberculosis, parasitism, and diarrheas in children predominated. These infectious diseases contributed to a high infant mortality rate. Following the Revolution, the leadership of the Ministry of Public Health decided to implement aggressive campaigns based on the fundamental principle of prevention in order to overcome some of these diseases in a short period of time (Beldarraín Chapel n.d.). Two of the most significant campaigns were directed against malaria and poliomyelitis. Because of their planning, implementation, and impact, these campaigns have served as examples for other developing countries in the Americas (Rojas Ochoa 2003).

THE PROGRAM TO ERADICATE MALARIA

After the Revolution and the creation of the new Ministry of Public Health, the leadership of the Ministry and of the country decided to fight against the infectious diseases that were the main causes of death for the Cuban population. Campaigns against malaria and poliomyelitis were instituted (Beldarraín Chapel n.d.).

The anti-malarial campaign started in February of 1959 with the founding of the Commission for Malarial Survey. In the same year an agreement with the Pan American Health Organization (PAHO) was signed. In 1959–1960,

the Commission for Malarial Survey began its initial efforts with the following tasks:

- Refine the legal basis for government management of this infectious disease;
- Establish international agreements;
- Search for cases in Cuba by conducting national field studies, demon-strations, and laboratory research to determine the location and exten-sion of the malarial areas;
- Notify public health officials of persons with fevers, accompanied by blood samples, establish a registry;
- Research malarial outbreaks;
- Test of anopheline susceptibility to DDT and Dieldrin;
- Define the malarial area or zone.

Legislation

Since 1908, when Health Ordinances of the Republic were drafted and
passed, article 238 stated that malaria was a disease of compulsory notification.

This aspect was confirmed by the Public Health Law of August 1, 1961
(Beldarraín Chapel n.d.).

On March 10, 1959, Decree-law 694 replaced the former Commission for
Malaria with the Commission for Malarial Survey as a branch of General
Health Division, and on April 21, 1959, Law 265 granted a financing credit
to this Commission.

Resolution 407 of May 18, 1959, established the compulsory cooperation of assistance and sanitary services of the Ministry of Public Health
(MINSAP) for taking blood samples from present or recent fever cases (Beldarraín Chapel n.d.).

On July 1, 1959, Law 844 stated that the Commission for Malarial Survey would be subordinated to the Communicable Disease Control Division
under the general executive management of MINSAP, as the newly reorganized Ministry of Health was called.

In August of 1960, the Commission reorganized into the National Service for Eradication of Malaria (NSEM) and retained this name until it was
incorporated into the General Health Services in March, 1967 (Beldarraín
Chapel n.d.).

International Agreements

The government of Cuba and PAHO/WHO (World Health Organization)
signed an agreement on February 26, 1959, to conduct the pre-eradication

survey and signed another agreement on August 26, 1960, to determine the operational plan and specify the responsibilities for both sides in undertaking the Program for the Eradication of Malaria.

On November 2, 1964, the Cuban government and PAHO/WHO signed an agreement on permanent advisory service from 1959 to 1966, and short-term consultancy, scholarships, equipment, and drugs for the treatment of cases from 1959 to 1971. The program also received the support of UNICEF in the form of vehicles and materials.

Searches for Cases at Home

In the period from May 22, 1959, to February 29, 1960, PAHO/WHO personnel participated in an initial survey to plan the campaign. In close cooperation with the National Medical College, a circular was sent to all the physicians in the country to request their cooperation; public health services, civil hospitals, and health facilities in sugar mills were visited; and some areas were selected for compulsory blood sampling of current and recent fever cases existing in municipalities with a history of malaria since 1948.

In addition, microscopic examinations of samples were conducted in situ, and if a sample was positive, then additional entomological analyses were undertaken, primarily to capture adult vectors and conduct larval screenings.

Three teams of three members each were dispatched for the fieldwork; a physician was the head of the team, accompanied by laboratory and entomological assistants. Also, an epidemiologist and an entomologist from PAHO/WHO accompanied the Cuban technicians and made a tour of all the municipalities located on the north and south coasts of Oriente province (Beldarraín Chapel n.d.).

Notification centers (862 in all) took blood samples from fever cases and other suspected cases. The samples were sent to the central laboratory of the Commission for parasitological examination.

The results of this active search were the following:

- Of the 111 municipalities in which blood samples were taken, 44 had positive cases (39.6 percent).
- Of the 1,603 localities where blood samples were taken, 157 of them had positive cases (9.7 percent).
- Of the 12,033 tested samples, 330 were positive, resulting in an index of positive plates or population prevalence rate of 2.7 percent.

The provinces that showed the highest positive percentage were Havana (12.2 percent) and Oriente (5.2 percent), with most of the cases found in Havana coming from people who had migrated from the province of Oriente.

Interestingly, 91 percent of the 330 positive samples belonged to *plasmodium vivax* and 9 percent to *plasmodium faciparum*, which is in contrast with the results of the malarial survey carried out in Cuba in 1936–1942 when the figures were 50 percent and 50 percent (Beldarraín Chapel n.d.).

The Commission for Eradication of Malaria studied four outbreaks, three of them located in the suspected malarial zone (Oriente and Havana provinces) and another one in Santiago de Cuba. These early initiatives revealed that Oriente province had the highest prevalence rate and the most generalized distribution of the disease, and this area represented an important source of infections for the rest of the island. These initiatives confirmed that malaria was not endemic in the rest of the island as was once hypothesized but rather was endemic only in Oriente province and a part of Camaguey province. The rest of the country witnessed outbreaks when epidemiological conditions were favorable in non-endemic areas.

With the technical cooperation of PAHO/WHO, all the localities in the malarial zone were mapped between January and July 1961 as follows—a sketch of each locality was made, houses were numbered, and a census on the quality of houses was conducted. Oriente province and the Alvaro Reynoso neighborhood in Camaguey were divided into forty sectors. The twenty sectors in the mountain areas in Oriente were mapped first; the other areas in the plains were selected to be mapped a second time during the rainy season.

A surveillance system was established in Oriente to perform the following tasks:

- Passive search for data;
- Active search if required from the epidemiological viewpoint;
- Immediate epidemiological research of all the detected cases;
- Treatment of all cases until their final recovery;
- Focal spray of positive houses and surroundings;
- Monthly follow-up with testing of blood samples from all detected cases.

The non-malarial zones also had an epidemiological surveillance service instituted and were divided into three regions: Region II comprising Camaguey and part of Las Villas; Region III part of Las Villas and Matanzas, and Region IV covering Havana and Piñar del Río. Each of these regions was followed up by a malaria expert and several assistants for evaluation of cases.

Cuba implemented a campaign of conventional measures in a program of eradication in Region I due to the prevalence of the infection. The expectation was that ending the transmission of the disease in the original province would eliminate the sources of cases in other provinces (Beldarraín Chapel n.d.).

Cuba's Program for the Eradication of Malaria began in 1959 and lasted until 1973. The creation of the National Health System made it possible to institute this program in four phases: preparatory phase, attack phase, consolidation phase, and the maintenance phase.

During the last stage, measures were set up to avoid the reintroduction of the disease in the national territory. Eight years after the program began in 1959, the last malarial case was reported. The year 1967 marked the end of malarial epidemics in Cuba. This last case was detected on June 28, 1967, in El Jobo, Nicaro, Mayarí region, under the then-Provincial Division of North Oriente (Beldarraín Chapel n.d.).

In September 1970, the Minister of Public Health requested that the PAHO director carry out the necessary studies for drawing up the final report that would allow the originally malarial area of the country to be included in the official WHO registry of areas in which malaria had been eradicated.

In the Eighth Report of the Expert Committee on Malaria, the eradication was defined as follows: "It can be considered eradicated when adequate surveillance operations do not permit to discover, after detailed screenings, any evidence of transmission or residual endemia for three years in a row and at least in the last years, there has been neither general measures of direct fight against anopheline vectors nor other operations that might have hidden the presence of residual foci" (*Documento de la OPS 1972* cited in Beldarraín Chapel n.d.).

A necessary requirement for keeping the disease eradicated was a surveillance system that identified the location of any case of malaria occurring in any place and at any time in an area under the phase of maintenance of eradication.

The selection of the type of surveillance in each sector was made based on an assessment of the receptibility of local population to the monitoring, the efficiency of the rural health services in the area, and the vulnerability of the population to the disease.

The technical operations of this surveillance program are summarized as follows:

- Localization of imported cases, cases that were not detected in the phase of consolidation despite an intensive search and cases of relapse after a radical treatment;
- Presumptive treatment of all suspected cases of malaria;
- Notification and treatment for final recovery of microscopically confirmed malarial cases;
- Immediate adoption of measures aimed at preventing or interrupting the transmission when a new case was observed in the receptive areas;
- Epidemiological study of confirmed cases of malaria to determine the origin of infection and determine the mode of transmission;

- Rapid adoption of adequate measures based on the results of the epidemiological studies to avoid the return of endemicity to the area;
- Preventive measures in receptive and vulnerable areas (WHO technical report 374, 32 in Beldarraín Chapel n.d.);
- Implementation of adequate measures against mosquitoes in border areas and in centers of concentration where groups from infested areas go (WHO Technical Report 272, 17 in Beldarraín Chapel n.d.).

The program was reevaluated in 1968, 1969, and 1970 with satisfactory results.

In summary, research studies conducted in 1959 started the anti-malaria campaign. Eight years later, the report of the last case of malaria marked the eradication of the disease. WHO announced that by 1967, Cuba had successfully eradicated malaria.

THE PROGRAM TO ERADICATE POLIOMYELITIS

Acute anterior poliomyelitis—polio—is a disease that primarily affects infants and children and causes serious disability. Dr. Francisco Cabrera Saavedra reported this disease for the first time in Cuba at the end of the Spanish domination when he found some people with the disease *sequelae* in Caibarién in 1898 (Beldarraín Chapel n.d.). American physicians also observed polio cases in the Isle of Pines in 1898. In 1909, Dr. Alberto Recio reported three cases of paralysis, two of which were caused by poliomyelitis. In the same year there was a report of the first epidemic outbreak in Las Villas province, with an incidence of 200 cases and a mortality rate of 8 percent, according to Dr. Martínez Fortún (Martínez-Fortún Foyo 1952 in Beldarraín Chapel n.d.), and 140 cases in 10 municipalities, according to a report submitted by Dr. Recio to Dr. Juan Guiteras, the local health director (Más Lago 1995, cited in Beldarraín Chapel n.d.). The report also indicated that this outbreak mainly affected children under four years of age.

In this context, one of the first steps taken by the post-revolutionary Ministry of Public Health was to control poliomyelitis epidemics in Cuba. In Cuba, epidemiological studies on poliomyelitis had been conducted on the history, development, and characteristics of the disease.

As a result of their understanding of the disease, Cuban health officials decided to carry out annual campaigns to control it. The strategy was based on three elements:

- High levels of vaccination coverage through one-week campaigns for each dose, before the high infection rates of the summer months;

- Surveillance of suspected cases;
- Foci-control actions if necessary.

After having assessed the problem appropriately and reviewing available scientific evidence that indicated that it was possible to eradicate the disease with the available material resources, campaign planning began in earnest in 1961. The goal was to vaccinate 80 percent of the population aged one month to fourteen years with trivalent oral Sabin vaccine; the total number of children at the time was estimated as 1,999,785 (Beldarraín Chapel n.d.). After a few months of planning, the campaign began in December of 1961 and lasted for six months. The campaign was carried out during two 15-day stages at six to eight week intervals. The first stage began on February 26, 1962.

The vaccination campaign was directed and controlled by the Ministry of Public Health with the support of mass block and brigade organizations like the Committee for the Defense of the Revolution (CDR). A National Coordinating Commission was set up and included the sub-secretary of Hygiene and Epidemiology, the sub-secretary of Medical Assistance, the president of the National Medical College, the president of the Red Cross, the president of the CDR, the Federation of Cuban Women, the Association of Young People from the Rebel Army, and the National Association of Small Farmers (ANAP). Its fundamental tasks were to engage the population in campaign activities, assist in raising people's awareness, overcome difficulties with families that might refuse vaccination, particularly in rural populations, and assure that all infants and children were brought to the vaccination posts.

The members of the National Commission of Anti-Polio Vaccination were officials from the Hygiene and Epidemiology sub-secretary and Medical Assistance respectively, under the direct advice of Dr. Karel Sacek, head of Epidemiology and Microbiology in Czechoslovakia and member of the Expert Committee in Virology from WHO (Beldarraín Chapel n.d.).

Each regional division established its own commission. The regional commissions coordinated and controlled the work in different units involved in the campaign as well as managed the vaccine storage and the distribution units. Regional director of public health, directors of hygiene and epidemiology, medical assistance, care of woman and child, the Provincial Council of Education, and the regional leaders of mass organizations participated in it (Beldarraín Chapel n.d.).

In each zone or division there was a municipal department in charge of coordinating and carrying out the vaccination program with the necessary amount of fixed and mobile equipment at its disposal. These departments were made up of the public health director of the zone, people in charge of Hygiene and Epidemiology and Medical Assistance, representatives of the Integrated Revolutionary Organizations (ORI), the Municipal Council of Education, and of mass organizations.

In the vaccination campaigns carried out in rural areas, the Social-Rural Medical Services, the farmers' militia troops, and the National Association of Small Farmers assumed special responsibilities.

All the required vaccines for immunization of the planned population were requested from the Ministry of Public Health of the USSR that sent them in two shipments according to each of the planned phases. They were transported and stored refrigerated to maintain the cold chain; 330,000 liquid vaccine doses were prepared for administration to children less than two years of age at each of the stages. The laboratory of the National Institute of Hygiene, Microbiology, and Epidemiology diluted the vaccine-candies to form by adding distilled water to a stable homogeneous suspension of pH 7.2, which was packed in 120 ml sterilized flasks containing an amount of suspension equal to 44 doses of 2.5 ml of vaccine (S/A 1962 cited in Beldarraín Chapel n.d.).

Anti-polio vaccines were sent from the central warehouse to seven Regional Commissions in refrigerated vehicles at -20°C. The vaccines were transported in refrigerators at 4–8°C from the Regional Commissions to the Zone Divisions in charge of distributing them among the vaccination centers with adequate means of transport.

The infant population was vaccinated as planned by administering a teaspoon of 2.5 ml of suspension to children less than two years of age and a vaccine candy to two- to fourteen-year-old children (Beldarraín Chapel n.d.).

The control and registry of doses were recorded in individual vaccination cards containing identity of each child, his address, the date of vaccine administration, doses, and signature of the responsible guardian.

The people in charge of the health component in the CDRs and members of ANAP registered all children aged one month to fourteen years from both urban and rural areas on the above-mentioned cards. Then the cards were given to the families so that they could deliver them in each vaccination center where they were alphabetically filed after the first stage to use them in the administration of a second dose to children. A documented proof of vaccination was given to the families to show that their children had been vaccinated (Beldarraín Chapel n.d.).

The vaccine card used by the vaccination centers was filled out after every child received the second dose. This served as an official model for recording the different types of vaccines that were administered.

Daily information from the vaccination centers reported the distribution by age groups and the number of liquid doses and vaccine candies provided. Daily reports were summarized at the zone division level, which were sent by phone to the regional division. Then data from the Vaccination Summarized Model at regional level were sent by phone to the Department of Statistics of the Ministry of Public Health on a daily basis.

The vaccination campaign was a multidisciplinary endeavor in which several state-run institutions and mass organizations worked in a coordinated way; such an effective result would not have been possible without their support. Additionally, for the first time in the history of the country, the people's participation was extremely important in attaining a public health-related goal (Beldarraín Chapel n.d.).

It appears as though the entire country of Cuba was involved in the polio eradication campaign. The Ministry of Education provided school premises to serve as vaccination centers as well as teachers who participated as members of vaccination teams. The Ministry of the Armed Forces lent helicopters for transporting vaccines and personnel in mountain regions and remote areas. The National Institute of Agrarian Reform placed refrigerated vehicles at the disposal of the campaign. The Committees for the Defense of the Revolution, the Federation of Cuban Women, Cuban Red Cross, the National Association of Young People from the Rebel Army, and the National Association of Small Farmers were responsible for fulfilling the following tasks in a coordinated way:

- Participation in the commissions at different levels;
- Active cooperation with vaccination propaganda and the creation of population awareness regarding the impact of the campaign;
- Transportation of children to the vaccination centers;
- Setting up commissions in charge of keeping public order, gathering statistical data, and other activities in favor of the massive campaigns;
- Control of children who were not vaccinated in the course of the national campaign;
- Control of vaccination cards where necessary data were collected as well as providing explanations to mothers so that they realized that it was important to take the vaccine cards to the vaccination centers;
- Collective surveillance.

The campaign was immensely labor intensive. The work force that performed the tasks during the campaign was divided into fixed teams and mobile teams. The fixed teams were composed of ten to fifteen people. One physician was the leader of the team and directed the actions. One person was in charge of transportation and administration of the vaccine, aided by two other persons. Another person was in charge of statistics, supervision and control of cards, preparation of listings of vaccinated children and of daily report models, which were given to zone divisions, and responsible for delivering documentary proofs of vaccination and vaccination cards. Another five to ten people were responsible for keeping order and closely watching the total ingestion of candies. The mobile teams were composed of five people. One was responsible for the equipment, a second was responsible for the vaccine, a third had responsibility for statistics, and two were in charge of maintaining public order (Beldarraín Chapel n.d.).

The educational component of the campaign was critical to its success, and it was extensive. Prior to the beginning of the campaign, the personnel were trained to work in the campaign at different levels throughout the country. Professor Karel Sacek gave lectures on poliomyelitis and oral live virus vaccines in several regional divisions and nationwide aimed at professionals and directors in the zones, while local professionals trained auxiliary staff (Beldarraín Chapel n.d.). In addition, 3,000 trainers of the people in charge of the health component of the mass organizations (CDR and others) received five-day courses at regional and national locations on oral anti-polio vaccination. In turn, these trainers trained 50,000 local people (Beldarraín Chapel n.d.).

At the same time, an intensive campaign of information and health education was disseminated on radio and television, including at least 30,000 vaccination announcements before and during the campaign and daily 12-minute television programs that featured talks, plays, lectures, and instructions regarding the anti-polio campaign. Two technical and two general information round tables were also broadcast on television in which national leaders of the campaign participated. A daily 30-minute radio program in the form of a play, aimed at the farmer population, was also broadcast. The population in different areas was informed of the vaccination campaign by means of mobile units from the Department of Health Education, and posters were given to the general public and to mothers, farmers, and children.

There was also an intensive press campaign involving newspapers, magazines, bulletins, and even billboards placed in cities and towns. Vaccination data were reported daily (Beldarraín Chapel n.d.). This early health promotion campaign presages the continued Cuban emphasis on the state role in health promotion. Simultaneously, the vaccination campaigns demonstrate the mechanisms by which the Cuban government so successfully encouraged and mandated community participation (Green 2003; Whiteford 1998, 2000).

Laboratory evaluation was undertaken that included the assessment of the child's immune condition by titration of neutralizing antibodies before and after each stage of the campaign. This serological control was repeated six months after the second stage as well (Beldarraín Chapel n.d.).

The following major objectives were achieved:

1. The goal of the anti-polio vaccination campaign was exceeded—87.5 percent of the population aged one month to fourteen years were vaccinated, with a performance rate of 109.4 percent of the initial goal of an 80 percent immunization rate.
2. The effectiveness of the participation of the population in such campaigns by giving adequate technical training to mass organizations was demonstrated.

3. The performance of the vaccination campaign was satisfactory in all age groups. The lowest percentage corresponded to the one-to-five-year-old group.
4. Once the vaccination campaign finished, the incidence of paralytic poliomyelitis was below the usual variation; only two cases occurred in May of 1962.
5. The results showed the effectiveness of two doses of one million TDC 50 trivalent vaccine for the protection of the Cuban population against poliomyelitis.
6. No side effects attributable to the vaccine were observed during the implementation of the campaign.

The statistical summaries of the campaign were reported as follows in tables 5.1–5.3 (including the slight discrepancies between tables; all data from Beldarraín Chapel n.d.):

Table 5.1.   Number of the first and second doses provided per province and the percentage rates of the second dose, Cuba, 1962

Province	Vaccination		
	First Dose	*Second Dose*	*% Compliance with Second Dose*
Pínar del Río	192,672	189,900	98.6%
Havana	520,757	477,767	91.7%
Matanzas	137,766	136,739	99.3%
Las Villas	372,373	360,938	96.9%
Camaguey	244,166	236,899	97.0%
Oriente	905,789	817,664	93.5%
CUBA	2,373,523	2,219,907	93.5%

Source: Adapted from Beldarraín Chapel n.d.

Table 5.2.   Antipoliomyelitic vaccination program second dose performance per province, Cuba, 1962

Province	Vaccination		
	Planned	*Performed*	*% of Planned*
Pinar del Río	173,124	189,900	109.7%
Havana	383,116	459,201	119.8%
Matanzas	131,840	134,570	102.1%
Las Villas	355,224	357,156	100.5%
Camaguey	207,649	232,397	111.9%
Oriente	748,832	814,631	108.8%
CUBA	1,999,785	2,187,855	109.4%

Source: Adapted from Beldarraín Chapel n.d.

Table 5.3. Antipoliomyelitis vaccination program second dose performance and achieved levels in the population by age groups, Cuba, 1962

Age Group	Population	Planned	Vaccinated Population	% of Population Vaccinated	% of Planned
1-11 months	202,685	162,143	193,912	95.7	119.6
1-5 years	942,242	753,790	754,858	80.1	100.1
6-14 years	1,354,805	1,083,842	1,239,085	91.4	114.3
TOTAL	2,499,732	1,999,758	2,187,855	87.5	109.4

Source: Adapted from Beldarraín Chapel n.d.

The impact of this vaccination campaign was clearly demonstrated because no more new cases occurred in the four months following the start of the campaign. Only 46 cases were reported in the first six months of 1962. After the first campaign, there was just a single poliomyelitis case in each of 1963, 1964, 1970, 1971, and 1972, and since May of 1962, there has been no polio mortality reported (Beldarraín Chapel n.d.).

There are still massive vaccination campaigns that are carried out within a 72-hour time frame, with over 90 percent coverage. From 1970 to 1992, the vaccination program consisted of two doses of trivalent vaccine at six-week intervals to be administered to children up to three years of age and a reactivation vaccine to be given to nine-year-old children. Family physicians and nurses participate in the campaign. Different vaccines with different presentation and potency have been used so far. This means that the vaccination campaigns have technically improved, which make it possible to keep the country free from the effects of the disease. This accomplishment was one of the first achievements of Cuban preventive medicine and epidemiology through the PHC (primary health care) model after the reform of the health care system in 1959. It allowed the country to obtain the International Certificate of Eradication granted by WHO in 1994 (Beldarraín Chapel n.d.).

From 1962 with the start of the campaign to 1994 when the international certificate of eradication was requested, 62,544,458 anti-polio vaccine doses were administered nationwide, thus ensuring a coverage rate higher than 90 percent of the Cuban population under forty-nine years of age (Más Lago 1995 as cited in Beldarraín Chapel n.d.). Several international organizations such as PAHO, WHO, and UNICEF cooperated with these campaigns.

When the vaccination program began in 1962, a National Commission for the Study of Infective Neurologic Syndromes was established, composed of neurologists, virologists, pediatricians, and epidemiologists. It was responsible for studying all suspected cases of poliomyelitis. From 1963 to 1989, it analyzed 93 suspected cases and confirmed 10 cases of poliomyelitis in non-vaccinated children. Non-poliomyelitic enteroviruses were isolated in 15 cases, whereas the remaining 68 were diagnosed with Guillain-Barré syndrome, myelitis transversa, or other polyneuropathies (Más Lago 1995 cited in Beldarraín Chapel n.d.).

The example of the Cuban polio eradication campaign highlights how PHC and its concomitant community participation component, worked together to control and then eradicate a deadly disease. Poliomyelitis was eradicated because the Cuban government established and then institutionalized a permanent combination of several elements critical to its success. They were a high level of immunization coverage, a highly sensitive and responsive surveillance system, a sustained political campaign, a high level of social participation, and effective health promotion.

Had the polio eradication campaign not been successful, more than 1,200 cases of paralysis and 200 deaths would have been expected to occur between 1962 and 1970 (based on the pre-1962 rates). The lives saved is another benefit of the campaign, but the campaign also served the purpose of strengthening the Cuban government's commitment to community-based PHC, without which the immunization campaigns could not have found the labor, skill, and expertise to accomplish their goals.

Dr. Mirta Roses, PAHO assistant director, vigorously applauded the Cuban vaccination campaign, saying: "Its conception, its ideology, its tools, its methodology shook the world. Cuba laid the fundamental basis for the big spark. Cuba changed probability into possibility" (Roses 1995:7 as cited in Beldarraín Chapel n.d.). Dr. Roses was present for the awarding of a certificate acknowledging the Cuban defeat of polio in 1995 (Beldarraín Chapel n.d.).

THE PROGRAM TO CONTROL DENGUE FEVER

Many countries in Central and South America—including Cuba—experienced an outbreak of dengue hemorrhagic fever (DHF) in 1981. Following the 1981 outbreak, Cuba instituted a rigorous and active environmental surveillance program in their attempt to control both dengue and dengue hemorrhagic outbreaks. It is a program dependent on their unique combination of PHC approaches.

Based on early detection, the Cuban government moved to implement an established source reduction action plan that was heavily dependent on trained human resources as well as the provision of economic resources. Fifteen thousand Cubans were pressed into service to combat the outbreak as inspectors, educators, and container retrieval and disposal agents. The environment surveillance program marshaled people as "vector controllers" to get rid of plants like bromeliads and other outdoor plants that collect water and serve as breeding grounds for the *aedes aegypti* mosquito, the primary vector for DHF. Others were trained to handle portable blowers to fog homes and still others to enforce sanitary laws concerning the disposal of outdoor water containers. At the same time, the government used airplanes to spray insecticide. This kind of mobilization of resources would only be possible when policies to combat such an outbreak had already been developed, plans designed to identify groups to support the effort, and people politicized and educated to the public health rationale behind the actions. In this instance, the previous programs to eradicate malaria and poliomyelitis in Cuba probably assisted in the smooth implementation of this program.

The three PHC strategies employed in the quick response and effective reduction of potential mortality rates were: environmental surveillance, health education, and an open hospitalization policy (Khouri et al. 1998). The health education campaign used mass media in a controlled market to distribute messages about dengue, its signs and symptoms, and its control. The educational campaign built upon previously established government-sponsored health education promotions with which the population was already familiar. Perhaps most importantly distinctive from other countries, such as the Dominican Republic, was the Cuban mechanism for engendering community response and support. Since the Cuban Revolution, efforts had been made to organize neighborhoods into politically active units. As with the poliomyelitis eradication case, these neighborhood brigades were marshaled in response to the dengue outbreak. Equally significant, the Cuban government created mobile field hospitals during the crises with a liberal policy of admissions. According to Khouri et al. (1998), almost 38 percent of all the reported cases were admitted and treated, thus reducing mortality rates significantly. According to official sources and outside observers, the Cuban response to the 1981 dengue outbreak was both innovative and effective (Guzman and Khouri 2002).

At the end of the 1981 dengue epidemic, Cuba also established a passive surveillance program, including testing suspected patients (ELISA). However, it is interesting to note that no positive cases were identified by this procedure.

In 1997 Cuba suffered another dengue outbreak with slightly more than 200 cases of DHF and almost 3,000 laboratory-confirmed cases of classic dengue fever (Khouri et al. 1998). Beginning with the 1997 outbreak, the active surveillance program was designed to identify cases early and trace the location of transmission. While there is some information to the contrary (Crabb 2001), Cuban data suggest that the early detection prevented the outbreak from spreading to the other 30 municipalities outside its initial site in Cuba. The passive surveillance initiated following the 1981 outbreak showed that mosquitoes were not found in patient's homes and that no indigenous transmission could be established from 1981 to 1996. It also suggested that reinfestation occurred in some areas, for instance in Santiago de Cuba (where the 1997 outbreak was centered) through the importation of tires transporting the *Aedes aegypti* vector in 1992.

The 1997 outbreak again gave rise to new surveillance techniques. Febrile patients at high risk in the primary health care system in the city of Santiago de Cuba were sought out for further testing between January and July of 1997. Sixty thousand emergency room patients were tested between November 1997 and January 1998. Home interviews also sought to identify febrile patients at high risk (Khouri et al. 1998). This combination of passive and active surveillance provided information about secondary infections related to mortality. Secondary infections were present in 100 of 102 (98 percent) of the dengue hemorrhagic and dengue shock cases.

There were 12 deaths, but no deaths under the age of sixteen. In the fatal cases, secondary infections were documented in 11 (92 percent) of the cases (Khouri et al. 1998). Dengue control, through both passive and active surveillance, was successful in reducing the severity and incidence of dengue in Cuba.

However, it is important to note that in the twenty years between 1981 and 2001, Venezuela reported 45,799 DHF cases compared to Colombia's 22,781 reported DHF cases and Cuba's 10,586 reported cases (PAHO 2002). Those rates are reflective of the estimated 2006 populations of those countries: 43.6 million in Venezuela, 25.7 million in Columbia, and 11.3 million in Cuba (CIA 2005). Thus, the systems that worked so well in Cuba apparently had equally as effective counterparts in other countries in the region.

THE PROGRAM TO CONTROL HIV/AIDS

Cuba applied the lessons it had learned with the malaria, polio, and dengue campaigns to their attempt to control one of the fastest growing diseases at the end of the twentieth century: human immunodeficiency virus (HIV)/acquired immunodeficiency syndrome (AIDS). In the midst of the worldwide HIV/AIDS pandemic, Cuba's 0.07 percent infection was among the lowest in the world (Zipperer 2005). According to a representative of PAHO, "Other countries can learn a lot from the Cuban system" (Zipperer 2005:400); they have managed HIV/AIDS through a national surveillance system that tracks both known cases and partners and provides free medical care, including Cuban-produced antiretroviral treatments, and extensive public health education and intervention. Cuba's HIV/AIDS public health program has been called "the most successful national AIDS programme in the world" (Burr 1997). According to the same author, it is also "the most hated AIDS programme in the world" (Burr 1997:647). What kind of program generates such conflicting opinions, and how did it develop in Cuba? Clearly some of these issues involved with the control of HIV/AIDS were significantly different from those Cuba encountered during its earlier malaria, polio, and dengue eradication campaigns.

Cuban health ministers attended a PAHO meeting on the growing world-wide epidemic of HIV/AIDS in 1983. Later that same year, even before their first documented case, Cuba implemented an extensive HIV surveillance program. In 1985 Cuba had its first documented case of AIDS (Hansen and Groce 2003:2875). In 1986, Cuba implemented a mandatory quarantine policy for people with HIV that included relocation to sanatoriums. In 1994, the quarantine was officially lifted. Nevertheless, in 2003, approximately half of all HIV-positive Cubans still lived in sanatoriums. Pregnant women with HIV are delivered by mandatory cesarean section to reduce the likelihood of transmission to the newborn. The net result was that Cuba's infection rate of 0.03 percent was one of the lowest in the world (Bentley 2003).

The practice of quarantining individuals with an infectious disease has long been a fundamental cornerstone of disease prevention in public health. Local health departments in the United States still rely on quarantines of children with certain infectious diseases like measles. Before the advent of the Salk vaccine to prevent poliomyelitis, children were preventively (and voluntarily) quarantined in their own homes and yards to minimize their exposure to the dreaded disease. Within the context of sexually transmitted diseases, the public health paradigm is routine testing, contact tracing, partner notification, medical surveillance, and partial social isolation.

But the initial Cuban model of mandatory quarantine, including relocation to a sanatorium for people with HIV and mandatory cesarean sections for pregnant women with HIV, generated a worldwide response from both public health experts and civil libertarians (Bentley 2003; Scheper-Hughes 1993; Hansen and Groce 2003; Parameswaran 2004). Some applauded the approach, others decried it. Often the reaction was predicated upon one's position on the balance between individual rights and conceptions of the common good, and on the role of the state.

Infectious diseases provide classic examples of rights in conflict. On the one hand, in the United States, the individual has a right to life, liberty, and the pursuit of happiness; is protected from unlawful search and seizure; and does not have to incriminate himself. On the other hand, governments—national, state, and local—have responsibilities for ensuring the health of the public. At times these rights and responsibilities are in conflict. When in conflict, many people differ on which of the two supersedes the other: the rights of the individual or the rights of the state.

The Cuban HIV/AIDS policy is both provocative and effective. According to Dr. Bryon Barksdale, a pathologist and director of the Cuba AIDS project, "The U.S. could learn from the Cuban HIV/AIDS policy" (Susman 2003:N7). When the Cuban Ministry of Health officials first learned of the impending AIDS epidemic, they banned the importation of blood derivatives from countries where blood banks were commercial enterprises ("capitalistic blood") where members of the population have been diagnosed with HIV/AIDS (Scheper-Hughes 1993). They also increased their own internal supply of blood to meet their needs, again relying on the public to comply with public health demands.

Commercial tests for HIV/AIDS became available in 1985, and Cuba immediately began the systematic testing of all Cubans who had been out of the country since 1981 (Scheper-Hughes 1993; Hansen and Groce 2003). This initial target group included a large number of Cuban military personnel who had participated in various campaigns in Africa during the 1980s. Cuban military personnel posted in Africa were among the early carriers of HIV/AIDS in Cuba. It is possible to speculate that the 1986 policy of mandatory isolation in special sanatoriums in part was possible because the target group was primarily military personnel. The military were among the first wave of HIV/AIDS cases in Cuba and, as military, were accustomed to being told where they could live (Parameswaran 2004). Because they were accustomed to following orders, perhaps they did not challenge the quarantine.

Cuba developed its own diagnostic kits in 1987 and began screening certain target groups, including all pregnant women, people with sexually transmitted diseases, all hospital inpatients, and all prisoners (Scheper-Hughes 1993; Parameswaran 2004). Even residents of entire neighborhoods, like Old Havana, a major tourist area, were screened for HIV/AIDS. But because screening, including blood screening, is so common in the Cuban health care system, the effect of this intensive screening may not have been considered unusual by many of the population (Scheper-Hughes 1993).

A total of 12 million HIV tests were performed in Cuba between 1985 and 1993, and the results indicate a very low prevalence of seropositive (HIV) people (fewer than 1,000), fewer than 200 total AIDS cases, and fewer than 125 new HIV cases per year (Scheper-Hughes 1993; Granich et al. 1995; Reed 2001). A 2001 article puts the 1999 estimate at approximately 1,500 seropositive people and suggests the rate doubled from 1995 to 1999 (Hsieh et al. 2001).

Twenty years after the first case of AIDS was identified in Cuba and after nearly as many years of extensive testing/surveillance, mandatory quarantines, and mandatory cesarean sections, what are the results? Nearly ten years after the first case, Scheper-Hughes reflected: "In France and Brazil thousands of people have been infected with HIV-contaminated blood and blood products; only 9 Cubans have been infected through a [blood] transmission." Puerto Rico, with one-third the population of Cuba, has more than 8,000 cases of AIDS, 208 of them in children. In Cuba, where only 200 people have AIDS, only one child has died of AIDS; three more carry the virus. In New York City, with roughly the same population as Cuba, 43,000 patients have AIDS" (1993:965).

But lest these results be attributed solely to the controversial HIV/AIDS program in Cuba, it is useful to remember that there was very little intravenous drug use in Cuba and very little tolerance of a gay lifestyle (Scheper-Hughes 1993; Zipperer 2005), which led to an exodus of gay Cubans in the 1970s and 1980s. In Cuba there is also easy access to abortion. Little intravenous drug use, intolerance of homosexuality, and free and accessible abortions tended to keep the rate of HIV/AIDS down in the 1990s and toward 2000.

While HIV transmission in Cuba through intravenous drug use or blood transfusions or to newborns at birth is low (Zipperer 2005), the increase in prostitution that resulted from the economic crisis of the 1990s poses a challenge to Cuba's effective HIV/AIDS program. Sex tourism has existed in Cuba, both before and after the Revolution. However, following the demise of the Soviet Union and its loss as a trading partner for Cuba, prostitution increased (Trumbull 2001:359). According to Trumbull, quoting an article by Julia O'Connell Davidson in *The Economist* in 2000: "In Cuba there is no network of brothels, no organized system of bar prostitution: in fact third party involvement in the organization of prostitution is rare" (Trumbull 2001:359). To which Trumbull adds that in Cuba, "Prostitutes are not sold into prostitution by their families and do not work in oppressive conditions as they do in other countries. They do not prostitute themselves because they are alcoholics or drug addicts. Most of the prostitutes interviewed decided to go into business on their own accord, driven by economic need" (2001:359). The actions of the *jineteras* (literally "jockeys or riders"; colloquially "sexual jockeys") to exchange sex for the chance to go out to eat, to dance, or for entertainment is not prostitution but an understood exchange. Without doubt, many jineteras also practice sex to increase their income and are paid for their services.

Prostitution in Cuba embodies one of the many Cuban conundrums: Prostitution is not illegal in Cuba, many Cubans do not consider sexual exchange immoral, money generated in the process helps individual Cubans, and the practice attracts tourists to the country. However, the government wants to control the practice as a means to contain raising HIV/AIDS rates (Trumbull 2001), and remove the conception of Cuba as a sex attraction. Given the success of the Cuban government's education and voluntary screening programs in controlling the spread of HIV/AIDS, Ministry of Health officials have argued against more repressive governmental interventions in dealing with the wide-spread practice of *jineterismo* (Waitzkin et al. 1997:14). Even with the government's previous success, the case of jineterismo and the transmission of HIV/AIDS provides another Cuban paradox between public health safety and individual economic initiative within a context of economic scarcity.

6

Primary Health Care and Chronic Diseases in Cuba

It is interesting to observe the processes and correlates of increasing life spans in developing and developed countries. For example, in the United States in 1900, life expectancy was approximately forty-seven years for men and forty-nine years for women. There were numerous causes of premature or preventable mortality—childbirth for women, mortality for newborns, and infectious diseases for children and adults. In fact, the categories of influenza and pneumonia, tuberculosis, and diarrhea, enteritis, and ulcerations of intestines accounted for approximately 30 percent of mortality at that time. By the year 2000, life expectancy in the United States had increased to seventy-four years for males and eighty years for females, and those same categories of infectious diseases that caused over 30 percent of the mortality in 1900 caused less than 3 percent in 2000 (USHHS 2002). Reductions in premature mortality due to childbirth and infectious diseases greatly increase life expectancy in all countries. But what happens when such causes of preventable mortality are in fact prevented? Then those members of the population who otherwise would have succumbed to one or another cause of preventable mortality live long enough to develop a plethora of chronic diseases that are associated with surviving to middle and older ages. As we will see, many of these chronic conditions are also preventable, but the model for prevention of chronic diseases is more complex than the model for the prevention of infectious or communicable diseases.

For Cuba, the transition from infectious disease mortality to chronic disease mortality was primarily accomplished during the interval between the 1959 Revolution—the start of Cuba's modern period—and the turn of the twenty-first century. Most epidemiologists, starting with Cuban epidemiologists, have concluded that there were no reliable or valid data on the actual health situation in the entire country prior to 1959. Customs, such as not registering the deaths of babies if the birth had not yet been recorded or was able to be rescinded, were commonplace. In that context, life expectancy in Cuba was estimated to be sixty years in 1960. Infectious diseases including malaria, polio, dengue fever, parasites, and tuberculosis contributed substantially to total mortality.

From a life expectancy of sixty years in 1960, life expectancy in Cuba soared to sixty-nine years in 1970 and seventy-seven years in 2003 (UNICEF 2005). In 2000, life expectancy in Cuba was estimated at seventy-five years for males and seventy-nine years for females, about the same as in the United States (United Nations Statistics Division 2005). Infant mortality was at 6 per 100,000 live births, compared to 7 per 100,000 for the United States.

The case of mortality attributable to acute diarrhea provides a good example of the changes in mortality patterns in Cuba during its modern era—the mortality rate dropped from 25.8 per 100,000 population in 1965 to 9.9 per 100,000 in 1973 and to 3.1 per 100,000 in 1980 (Valdes 2001).

Accompanying this remarkable decline in preventable infectious disease mortality was the rise in chronic health conditions in those fortunate enough to live into middle and old age. In Cuba in 2000, the five leading causes of death were cardiovascular disease, malignant neoplasms (cancers), cerebrovascular diseases (strokes), accidents, and influenza and pneumonia, with the first three accounting for 60 percent of all deaths (PAHO 2005). For comparison, in the United States the five leading causes of death in 2000 were diseases of the heart, malignant neoplasms, cerebrovascular diseases, chronic lower respiratory diseases, and accidents, with the first three accounting for 59 percent of all deaths (Anderson 2002).

Although cardiovascular diseases are the leading cause of mortality in Cuba in 2000 with 180.3 deaths per 100,000 population (PAHO 2005), both Cuba and the United States are experiencing reductions in the mortality rates attributable to cardiovascular disease. In the United States, the decline has been steady since the 1950s. For Cuba the decline probably began in 1970 and has been apparent since 1990 when the age- and sex-adjusted mortality rates attributable to cardiovascular diseases were approximately 171 deaths per 100,000 and declined to approximately 133 per 100,000 by 2000 (the crude rate of 180.3 obtained from PAHO for 2000 is not inconsistent with an age- and sex-adjusted rate of 133 for 2000 because of the adjustments). This reduction in cardiovascular mortality is generally considered to be the result of earlier detection of cardiovascular diseases (secondary prevention), better treatment (tertiary prevention), and advances in the primary prevention of the onset of the diseases themselves (healthy lifestyles such as regular physical activity, healthy eating, and the avoidance of tobacco use).

When the life expectancy in a country is forty to fifty years, much of the mortality is typically caused by infectious and communicable diseases that are eminently preventable. When life expectancies are seventy to eighty years, much of the mortality is typically caused by certain chronic diseases—cardiovascular diseases and malignant neoplasms in particular—that are also largely preventable as well. Furthermore, life expectancies below fifty years are more common in developing countries, while life expectancies greater than seventy years are more common in developed countries. Cuba is an exception. By most economic indicators, it is a developing country. But by most health indicators, it is a developed country.

CARDIOVASCULAR DISEASES

Let us begin with some clarification of terms. Cardiovascular disease is a general term referring to any number of specific diseases that affect either the heart (i.e., the cardiac muscle) or the vessels (i.e., arteries) that transport the oxygenated blood pumped by the heart. Vascular diseases that restrict blood flow through the arteries caused most commonly by fatty deposits inside the walls of the arteries are one form of cardiovascular disease. A diminished capacity of the heart muscle itself, such as faulty valves, blocked aorta, and overstrain, is another. Vascular restrictions in turn strain the heart muscle to overcome the resistance in the peripheral arteries or in the pulmonary (lung) circulation. Ischemia is manifested in the various tissues that are not getting a sufficient supply of oxygenated blood due to blockages. A long-lasting or chronic insufficiency of the oxygenated blood can lead to necrosis or death of the tissue.

Fatty deposits on the insides of the arteries can dislodge and travel through the arteries to cause additional blockage that reduces blood flow and oxygen delivery, resulting in tissue death. A myocardial infarction is another term for a heart attack, which in its simplest form means the rapid death of a portion of the heart tissue. A myocardial infarction is typically an acute complication of ischemic heart disease.

Hypertension is a disease end-point in and of itself, while at the same time it is also a primary risk factor for more lethal forms of cardiovascular disease such as ischemic heart disease. Hypertension is the elevation in tension measured by arterial blood pressure. Higher pressure means that the heart muscle has to work harder to get the blood flowing to all the tissues in the body. Obesity increases the load on the heart, because obesity disproportionately increases the body size and therefore the heart has a greater volume of tissues to support with oxygen. At the same time, obesity is often caused by eating excessive amounts of fatty foods and processed sugars that increase serum lipid levels and can thereby facilitate the accumulation of

plaque inside the arterial walls. Obesity makes it difficult for the individual
to engage in physical activity sufficient to raise the heart rate safely enough
to lead to increased cardiovascular fitness. Many of these terms are interre-
lated, and that is why cardiovascular disease can be considered the broadest
term.

Ischemic heart disease is by far the most serious and among the most common form of cardiovascular disease. Among those aged thirty-five and over
in Cuba, ischemic heart disease caused more than 15,000 deaths in 2000,
with a rate of 341.5 per 100,000 among males and 248.3 per 100,000 among
females (WHO 2003b). A recent article by Alberto Hernández Cañero, director of the Cuban Institute of Cardiology and Cardiovascular Surgery, offers
insight into the rise and fall of ischemic heart disease mortality in Cuba
(1999). Figure 6.1 presents the mortality rates from ischemic heart disease in

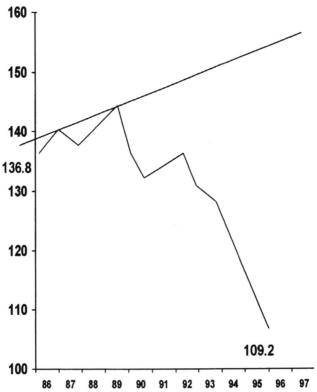

Figure 6.1. Mortality Rates from Ischemic Heart Disease in
Cuba, 1986–1997, adjusted to the 1981 population. Adapted from
*La Dirección Nacional de Estadística del Ministerio de Salud
Pública de Cuba* 1999.

Cuba from 1986 to 1997 (adjusted to the 1981 population) provided by the National Statistics Division of the Ministry of Public Health in Havana. The trend from 1986 to 1990 shows a steady and alarming rate of increasing mortality, peaking with a rate of 144.8 per 100,000. Then from 1990 through 1997, there is a dramatic decline, culminating in a rate of 109.2 per 100,000. That drop represents a 25 percent decrease in just seven years from the peak rate in 1990.

Much is known about the causes and antecedents of ischemic heart disease. Diet directly influences a person's serum cholesterol. The dietary consumption of high levels of saturated fats and cholesterol are associated with higher levels of serum lipids and cholesterol. Higher levels of serum cholesterol, in turn, are associated with higher rates of atherosclerosis. In fact, the Framingham Heart Study had demonstrated as early as 1977 that a reduction of 5 mg/dl in serum cholesterol over six years was associated with a 4.3 percent decrease in this type of cardiovascular disease. Public health offices in the United States and other developed countries with high rates of cardiovascular disease mortality have had campaigns to get their citizens to eat "heart healthy" and thereby to reduce their serum cholesterol and lipid levels.

In 1987 Ríos and Tejeiros reported changes in the caloric and protein consumption of the Cuban people beginning in 1965. In the approximately twenty years covered by their analysis, they reported that the Cuban people increased their total caloric intake by 15.7 percent, increased their total protein intake by 19.8 percent, and increased their animal protein intake by 25.2 percent.

However, 1990—the zenith of ischemic heart disease mortality in Cuba—was also shortly before the beginning of a "special period" in Cuba that began after the Soviet Union announced it was ending economic support to Cuba. The former Soviet Union previously accounted for approximately 85 percent of Cuba's international trade. These economic hardships were exacerbated by the tightening of the 30-year-old economic embargo initially imposed by the United States shortly after Fidel Castro disposed of the Cuban dictator, Batista. This "special period" was truly an economic crisis, marked by drastic reductions in the importation of staples like food, medicines, and oil that Cuba had relied on the former Soviet Union to provide. At the same time, Cuba was ill prepared to become self-sufficient in these areas overnight, and so people were forced to change their dietary habits. In the short run, the health of the Cuban population was at risk, with nearly 50,000 people affected by the epidemic of neuropathy between 1991 and 1993 (Hernández Cañero 1999). However, Hernández Cañero was able to compare the total serum cholesterol levels of samples of Cubans before and after 1990. Based on 1988 data from a population survey in Havana, 29 percent of men and 38 percent of women had levels of total serum cholesterol higher than 5.2 mmol/l, with a mean level of 5.3 mmol/l (204.6 mg/dl).

Remarkably, a 1994 survey in Havana demonstrated that the mean level of total serum cholesterol decreased substantially to 4.2 mmol/l (163.6 mg/dl) (Hernández Cañero 1999). Another study, this time among Cuban railway workers conducted in 1987 and 1988 found that 15 percent of both men and women had total serum cholesterol levels greater than 6.2 mmol/l (240 mg/dl), but a comparable study conducted in 1995 found that the total serum cholesterol levels was 3.5 mmol/l in men and 3.3 mmol/l in women (Hernández Cañero 1999).

Whether a diet lower in saturated fats—consistent with a healthy heart diet—will continue among the Cuban people after the economic crisis of the "special period" remains to be seen.

Another consequence of the withdrawal of economic supports by the former Soviet Union and the heightened economic embargo imposed by the United States was the reduction in petroleum supplies in Cuba, which in turn meant shortages of gasoline. This resulted in an increase in walking, bicycling, and other forms of physical activity among the Cuban population. Increased physical exercise, of course, is another important health promotion/disease prevention activity repeatedly demonstrated to increase fitness and reduce cardiovascular disease and mortality.

Hypertension is a health problem in Cuba, just as it is in most developed countries. The Cuban National Health System has signaled hypertension for special attention. Whereas many developed countries approach control of hypertension with pharmacologic agents, Cuba relies extensively on the lifestyle prescription of diet and exercise encouraged by its more than 28,000 family doctor and nurse teams.

Several studies implemented in different locations across Cuba during the last 20 years have estimated that approximately 30 percent of the urban population and 15 percent of the population in rural areas suffer from hypertension (blood pressure over 140/90 mmHg) (Pérez Caballero et al. 2000). Some studies have suggested that Cubans with a greater African heritage have higher rates of arterial hypertension than Cubans with a greater European heritage, but such findings are problematic because race differentiation in Cuba is not clear (Pérez Caballero et al. 2000).

Cuban researchers have reported successes in reducing the rates of arterial hypertension (Pérez Caballero et al. 2000). An intervention trial in the province of Cienfuegos was credited with reducing prevalence from 44 percent to 39 percent. WHO guidelines suggest that a 2 percent decrease in average arterial blood pressure in a specified population should result in 6 percent decrease in the annual mortality rate from cerebrovascular accidents (i.e., strokes) (Pérez Caballero et al. 2000).

CANCERS

Table 6.1 presents the WHO's published rates (and last updated in December, 2004) of all cancer mortalities in Cuba for males and females from 1964 through 1996, indicating the number of deaths, crude mortality death rate per 100,000 population, and age-standardized rates (WHO 2004). The population in Cuba was getting older during this interval, and cancer affects older people more frequently than younger people, so the crude mortality rates show steady increases in mortality, but age-adjusted rates show a slight decline from 1970 (132.5 for males and 96.1 for females) to 1996 (127.4 for males and 93.6 for females) (WHO 2004). The relatively abrupt and dramatic changes between 1969 and 1970 for both males and females are in all likelihood attributable to changes in measurement procedures rather than to dramatic changes in the actual rates themselves.

Italian and Swiss researchers (Bosetti et al. 2005) recently published a paper comparing the gender-specific and age-adjusted death rates for fourteen different cancers for eleven countries and one territory in the Americas (including all three from North America (Canada, Mexico, and the United States); three from Central America/the Caribbean (Costa Rica, Cuba, and Puerto Rico); and six from South America (Argentina, Brazil, Chile, Colombia, Ecuador, and Venezuela). The data summarized in table 6.2 are from the year 2000, except for Brazil (1995), Chile (1999), and Colombia (1999).

Using a world standardization technique eliminates the influence of differences in age and sex distributions across countries and thereby allows for comparisons across countries but unfortunately renders the rates themselves difficult to interpret within a country. We observe first that total cancer mortality for men in the United States was ranked fourth among the

Table 6.1. Cancer Mortalities in Cuba, 1964–1996

	Female				*Male*		
Year	*Deaths*	*Crude Rate*	*Age Standardized Rate*	*Year*	*Deaths*	*Crude Rate*	*Age Standardized Rate*
1965	3,096	80.8	127.3	1965	4,688	117.9	187.9
1970	3,349	80.4	96.1	1970	5109	116.6	132.5
1975	3,790	83.0	98.6	1975	5,451	114.4	128.5
1980	4,266	89.5	94.9	1980	6,150	123.9	124.9
1985	4,892	99.3	95.0	1985	6,901	135.0	124.7
1990	5,712	108.3	93.7	1990	7,940	148.9	127.4
1995	6,132	112.3	91.0	1995	8,484	154.2	127.0

Source: Adapted from the World Health Organization 2004.

Table 6.2.   Male and female site-specific cancer mortality rates per 100,000 for eleven countries and one territory in the Americas in 2000, indicating the highest ranked rate and the lowest ranked rate to establish ranges and Cuba's rank and rate and the United States' rank and rate standardized to worldwide ages

	United States		Cuba		
	Mortality Rate[1]	Rank[2]	Mortality Rate[1]	Rank[2]	Highest–Lowest
Males					
All cancers	146.41	4	138.71	5	155.98–84.86
Lung	46.92	1	38.29	3	46.92–7.71
Stomach	3.65	12	6.86	10	33.75–3.65
Prostate	12.73	11	23.06	1	23.06–11.95
Intestines	13.96	3	10.46	5	15.43–3.42
Leukemia	5.94	1	4.36	6	5.94–3.61
Esophagus	4.98	5	4.52	7	7.99–1.89
Mouth/Pharynx	2.73	6	5.74	2	6.64–1.35
Larynx	1.62	11	7.26	1	7.26–0.90
Bladder	3.65	4	4.00	3	4.61–0.98
Testis	0.21	10	0.28	9	1.30–0.20
Bone	0.41	12	1.27	1	1.27–0.41
Females					
All cancers	105.38	3	102.86	4	113.65–75.30
Lung	26.21	1	16.72	3	26.21–3.80
Stomach	1.84	12	3.52	9	13.68–1.84
Breast	17.56	3	14.82	4	20.65–6.97
Uterus	4.59	11	14.13	4	16.92–3.79
Intestines	9.82	2	12.48	1	12.84–3.65
Leukemia	3.58	1	3.35	4	3.58–2.73
Ovary	5.84	1	3.35	8	5.84–2.26
Esophagus	1.09	8	1.40	4	3.53–0.57
Mouth/Pharynx	0.98	7	1.48	1	1.48–0.48
Larynx	0.35	7	1.23	1	1.23–0.13
Bladder	1.15	2	1.15	3	1.20–0.62
Bone	0.26	12	1.14	2	1.22–0.26

Source: Adapted from Bosetti et al. 2005
[1]Per 100,000
[2]Among eleven countries and one U.S. territory

countries and third for women, while in Cuba men had the fifth highest cancer mortality among the countries surveyed and Cuban woman were fourth. For lung cancer, by far the most lethal of all malignant neoplasms, both men and women from the United States had the highest rates of any of the countries; Cuban men and women were third. For breast cancer among women, the United States was ranked third and Cuba fourth. For prostate cancer among men, Cuba was ranked first and the United States eleventh at about half the rate (23.06 versus 13.14). Cancer of the intestines—primarily of the colon and the rectum—was fifth among Cuban men and first among Cuban women, compared to third among American men and second among American women. Overall, Cubans fare slightly better, that is, have slightly lower cancer mortality rates, than their counterparts in the United States. The notable exceptions to that statement are that Cuban men have almost twice the rate of prostate cancer mortality than men in the United States, and men and women in the United States have the highest rates of lung cancer of any of the countries, while Cuba's men and women were ranked third. The last anomaly was the difference in intestinal cancer rates between Cuban men (fifth) and Cuban women (first).

It may be significant to note that Cuba has the highest rate for mouth, pharynx, and larynx cancers, something associated with smoking. One of the apparent contradictions in the Cuban cancer data is the relatively low rate of lung cancer at the same time as high levels of smoking. Perhaps smokers are lost to the population through fatalities associated with mouth, pharynx, and larynx cancers before they can present with lung cancer.

The trends over time (1970–2000) provided by the Italian and Swiss researchers suggest that rates of cancer mortalities overall—lung, breast, prostate, and intestine cancers in particular—are generally declining slightly in the United States while increasing in Cuba (overall, lung, prostate, and intestine) or level (breast cancer) (Bosetti et al. 2005). The age-adjusted rate of cancer of the lung/trachea/bronchus in the United States has been steadily dropping for men since 1990, but unfortunately is increasing for women.

In 1984 another study from Cuba examined the association between smoking the local dark tobacco and lung cancer employing a retrospective case control design among hospitalized cases with cytological and/or histological confirmation of lung cancer, and both hospital and neighborhood controls (Joly, Lubin, and Caraballose 1984). After reporting that the overall relative risk of lung cancer among females who ever smoked regularly was 7.3 and for males who ever smoked regularly was 14.1, the authors pointed out that 76 percent of female lung cancer cases had reported that they ever smoked cigarettes regularly, while 98 percent of the male cases did. It was particularly interesting to note that the authors reported that ap proximately 31 percent of the female controls and 80 percent of the male controls also reported that they ever smoked cigarettes regularly.

Comparable research in the United States typically examines the association between current smokers and lung cancer to determine a relative risk rate. But other researchers have examined relative risks for former smokers and passive smokers as well. What intrigued us about these findings reported from Cuba by Joly and colleagues (1984) were the rates of "ever smoking regularly" which is typically defined as smoking 100 cigarettes or more in one's lifetime as contrasted with those who "never smoked regularly," typically defined as smoking fewer than 100 cigarettes in one's lifetime. Female cases had a 76 percent rate and female controls had a 31 percent of "ever smoking regularly."

Assuming equal numbers in both groups, those rates translate into a mean smoking rate of approximately 50 to 55 percent for females in Cuba in 1983. The comparable rates for males were 98 percent of cases and 80 percent of controls for a mean smoking rate of close to 90 percent. Comparable prevalence rates from the United States National Health Interview Survey of Noninstitutionalized People indicated that 67 percent of men and 46 percent of women aged twenty years and older reported "ever smoked regularly" (National Center for Health Statistics 1984:86). Inferring then that many more men from Cuba can be categorized as "ever smoked regularly" than men in the United States (90 percent versus 67 percent), it is interesting to observe that cancer rates reported in table 6.2 indicate that U.S. lung cancer mortality rates are about 20 percent higher for both men and women compared to Cuban lung cancer mortality rates. Admittedly the "ever smoking regularly" rates were estimated from 1983, while the cancer mortality rates in Table 6.2 are from 2000, but findings of higher smoking prevalence rates in Cuba coupled with higher lung cancer mortality rates in the United States invite speculation.

Perhaps poor air quality disadvantages the U.S. population and contributes to higher lung cancer rates, notwithstanding the conclusion of the authoritative work by Doll and Peto published in 1981 that contends that only 1 to 2 percent of lung cancer deaths are attributable to air pollution and also notwithstanding the assertion of the U.S. Centers for Disease Control and Prevention that 88 to 91 percent of lung cancer deaths among males in the United States are due to cigarette smoking and 68 to 78 percent among women (1993). Perhaps genetic and constitutional differences attributable to ethnicity might explain these findings. Perhaps treatment differences affect mortality rates but not incidence rates, notwithstanding that lung cancer is one of the most difficult cancers to treat (American Cancer Society 2005).

The three-year survival rate in Cuba is 11 percent and the five-year survival rate in the United States is 15 percent. Perhaps there is more to be understood about possible excess rates of lung cancers attributable to the pesticides and additives that the U.S. tobacco industry adds to tobacco leaves during cultivation and processing. According to the American Cancer Society, "Cigarettes, cigars, and smokeless and pipe tobacco consist of tobacco leaves, as well as ingredients added for flavor and other properties. More than 4,000 individual compounds have been identified in tobacco and tobacco smoke, including more than sixty compounds that are known carcinogens (cancer-causing agents)" (American Cancer Society 2005). Perhaps the apparent excess lung cancer mortality in the United States compared to Cuba may be linked to differences in the methods of cultivation and processing of tobacco products.

At this point another issue comes to mind: What is the Cuban government doing to curtail cigarette smoking, and therefore the excess rates of cancers attributable to smoking, among its population? Having noticed that the ubiquitous billboards supporting one socialistic position or public health exhortation seemed to be missing any mention of the harmful effects of cigarette smoking, Branch pursued the topic informally with some Cubans in a mid-sized urban area. He approached one man he knows quite well—approximately forty years old, a manual laborer, and a cigarette smoker—and asked him if there were any government programs that urged Cubans not to smoke cigarettes. His response should be encouraging to the health ministry. The man responded that there are weekly television programs on which a physician presents one of three health messages. One is to practice safe sex, a second is to only drink alcohol in moderation and never to drive after drinking, and the third is that cigarette smoking is harmful. It was impressive that the proverbial man on the street could report these important public health messages.

In addition, the national cigarette packages have a variety of targeted, large print, direct messages on the panels that are more specific than the U.S. Surgeon General's warning on the side panel of U.S. cigarettes (see photograph 6.1). The messages are:

- Protect Your Family From Tobacco
- Help Your Children By Not Smoking
- If You Smoke During Pregnancy You Will Harm Your Baby
- Everyone Deserves Clean Air

These are strong health education messages from the government that cigarette smoking is a serious health hazard. At the same time, Cuban cigarettes are inexpensive and widely available. It was interesting to observe, however, that no comparable messages are put on the cigars produced for Cuban consumption.

What are we to infer from these cancer mortality data for Cuba? Specific data on both the incidence (the number or rate of new cases) and mortality rates are available for prostate cancer from 1977 through 1999 (Galán Alvarez et al. 2004). During this interval, the incidence rates went up 11 percent for those under age fifty, up 27 percent for those aged fifty-one to sixty-four years of age, and up 23 percent for those aged sixty-five and over. At the same time, mortality rates stayed flat for those under age fifty; rates increased dramatically by 63 percent for those aged fifty-one to sixty-four and even more dramatically by 82 percent for those aged sixty-five and over.

Photograph 6.1. This collage depicts the common warnings displayed on Cuban cigarettes in 2005; notice that the warning is in large print on a whole panel, not in small print on a side panel as in the United States; from the top clockwise, the different messages are "Protect your family from tobacco," "If you smoke during pregnancy you may harm your baby," and "Help your children not to smoke."

While in many places mortality rates for many cancers are decreasing due to more aggressive and better treatments, this trend does not seem to appear in Cuba. However, it should be added that treatments for prostate cancer have not improved as much as some other interventions. Data could not be located on the incidence, mortality, and survival data for cancer sites in addition to the prostate.

To clarify incidence-mortality-survival phenomena more carefully, we obtained three-year survival rates for a variety of cancers reported to the National Cancer Registry of Cuba in 1988–1989 (Graupera Boschmonar et al. 1999). In Cuba, women with breast cancer had the highest rates of three-year survival at 62 percent; prostate survivors were 45 percent at three years, colon cancer survival was 38 percent at three years, and lung cancer three-year survival was down to 11 percent. The most comparable figures we were able to obtain for the United States were five-year survival rates for the 1992–1998 interval; for breast cancer five years survival was 88 percent, prostate survivors were 98 percent, colon cancer survivors were 67 percent, and lung cancer survivors were 15 percent. With the exception of lung cancer, the survival rates are much higher in the United States, and the cancer survival rates continued to improve during the 1990s (United Kingdom 2005).

The overall implications of incidence-mortality-survival cancer rates in Cuba suggest that more rather than fewer resources may be needed to treat cancers in Cuba during the coming decades, and that renewed efforts for primary prevention may be necessary to stem rising rates.

CEREBROVASCULAR ACCIDENTS/STROKES

We found surprisingly little data on cerebrovascular accidents (strokes) from Cuba or about Cuba, notwithstanding that cerebrovascular diseases are the third most common cause of death in Cuba. One article and an editorial in 2000 reported that the rates of cerebrovascular accidents had risen precipitously in 1999 (Table 6.3) (Delgado Zapata, Valdespino Llerena, and Malpica Selleck 2000; Santiago Luis and Delgado Zapata 2000).

For the purpose of comparison, crude death rates per 100,000 population for all ages in the United States were 40.3, 40.8, and 34.0 for 1996, 1997, and 1998 (USDHHS 2002).

Table 6.3. Rates of cerebrovascular accidents per 100,000 population in Cuba.

Year	1996	1997	1998	1999
Rate	72.3	69.3	71.0	75.4

Source: Adapted from Delgado Zapata et al. 2000

In Cuba, women over age sixty-five had the highest death rates of cerebrovascular accidents, almost 50 percent higher than men over age sixty-five. The gender differential is not as great in the United States. But the editorial by Luis Santiago et al. 2000 pointed out that the cerebrovascular accidents had begun to be problematic even among those under age fifty in Cuba. Furthermore, risk factors for cerebrovascular accident mortality in Cuba, in addition to age, include diabetes, smoking tobacco, and the combination of alcoholism and tobacco smoking.

Other published studies about cerebrovascular accidents in Cuba include one retrospective descriptive study of the characteristics and comorbidities of 198 decedents from one province (Domínguez Alvarez et al. 1999). Another study examined 897 decedents from a single hospital, using both medical histories and autopsies to clarify correlates of death (Olivia Linares et al. 2001). The primary finding of this study was that arterial hypertension was the most frequent risk factor observed among the decedents. Yet a third study examined the epidemiology of cerebrovascular accidents in Cuba by examining a prospective cohort of 1,369 people aged fifteen or older in the specific province of Cienfuegos (Álvarez Li 1998). Unfortunately, this study was underpowered, having had too few subjects to make it reliable and allow valid inferences about risk factors. A fourth study reported on 79 patients discharged from the Instituto Nacional de Neurología in Havana, with again too few subjects to provide insights beyond clinical experiences (Fernández Concepción et al. 2002).

DIABETES

Although not one of the five leading causes of death in Cuba or the United States (it is 6th in both countries), *diabetes mellitus* (DM), a disease of older populations in developed countries, can reasonably be expected to be part of Cuba's chronic disease future. Furthermore, the causes of death in a population do not match precisely with the conditions the population lives with. For example, a recent probability survey in Old Havana reported prevalence rates of noncommunicable chronic diseases as 26 percent for hypertension, 11 percent for diabetes mellitus, 10 percent for ischemic heart disease, 6 percent for bronchial asthma, and 4 percent for hypercholestelemia among people aged sixty and older in 1994–1996 (Victoria, Torres Páez, and Astrain Rodríguez 1999).

Diabetes is similar to hypertension in that both are serious diseases in their own rights, and at the same time, both are important risk factors for even more serious chronic diseases, particularly ischemic diseases of the heart, brain, eyes, kidneys, and the peripheral arterial vascular system. Diabetes mellitus in essence represents an inability of the body to process glu-

Table 6.4.   Incidence of diabetes mellitus per 1,000 by age and sex, Cuba, 1992–2001

	Males		Females	
Age Group	*1992*	*2001*	*1991*	*2001*
Under 15 years	0.05	0.09	0.05	0.09
15–24 years	0.28	0.46	0.33	0.52
25–59 years	0.78	1.53	1.28	2.37
60 years and older	3.86	5.34	5.55	8.11
Totals	0.97	1.57	1.50	2.47

Source: Adapted from López Nistal and Álverez 2005

cose (sugars). Incorrect processing can occur either because the body does not produce enough insulin to metabolize the glucose or because the body does not metabolize correctly the insulin it produces. Typically the form of diabetes characterized by insufficient production of insulin occurs early in life, and has been called Type 1 or early onset diabetes/childhood diabetes. The other form, often called Type 2, generally occurs later in life and is often associated with obesity.

In the United States, there has been a surprising increase in Type 2 diabetes among younger people, suggesting that the epidemic of obesity in the United States is taking one of its tolls on the younger people in the form of early onset of Type 2 diabetes.

A recent report indicated that incidence rates (new cases) of DM in Cuba have risen rapidly between 1992 and 2001 (López Nistal and Álvarez 2005). Table 6.4 demonstrates that the incidence of DM rose over 60 percent in both males and females during that ten-year period. There were substantial increases within each of the age groups as well, suggesting that the pandemic of DM has not escaped Cuba. Additional information suggests that most of the increase came after 1996.

The same article also pointed out that the prevalence rates (the total of new and old cases) of DM also rose about the same amount during that interval, from 11.8 to 18.3 per 1,000 for men and from 20.7 to 32.3 per 1,000 for women. The surprising finding, however, was that the mortality rates due to DM went up 66 percent among men from the 1980–1984 base interval to the 1992–1996 interval, but then went down 31 percent from 1992–1996 to 1997–2001. The findings were even more dramatic for women—their mortality rates went up 81 percent from 1980–1984 to 1992–1996, then went down 34 percent between 1992–1996 and 1997–2001 (López Nistal and Álvarez 2005).

Because DM is a chronic condition, once a person is diagnosed with it, that person always has it, even if the diagnostic indicators of DM are under control for the individual and below diagnostic threshold. The implication from the rising incidence and prevalence rates of DM in Cuba but declining mortality rates is that the people in Cuba with DM are not dying from it as often as people did in the past. This conjecture, in turn, implies that perhaps treatment in Cuba is more effective than it was in the past.

A recent study of diabetes education among the Cuban elders addresses this issue and seems to capture the quintessential approach and success of the Cuban PHC model (García and Suárez 1996). Enrolling 148 diabetic patients aged sixty years or over to participate in monthly educational efforts over a five-year period, the attempt was to empower patients with knowledge, attitudes, and practices to cope with diabetes, and metabolic control (like diet) was emphasized rather than clinical aspects of the disease. The pre- and post-intervention results demonstrated a significant increase in knowledge and skills for self-care treatment as well as significant reductions in body weight and anti-diabetic medications (specifically daily doses of insulin and oral compounds). Over the course of the trial, both emergency services and hospital admissions related to diabetes care were reduced. In addition, *HbA1c* levels also improved significantly.

The "Hb" in HbA1c means hemoglobin, the compound in the red blood cells that transports oxygen. Hemoglobin occurs in several variants; the one that composes about 90 percent of the total is known as hemoglobin A. A1c is a specific subtype of hemoglobin A. The 1 is actually a subscript to the A, and the c is a subscript to the 1. Glucose binds slowly to hemoglobin A, forming the A1c subtype. In non-diabetic persons, the formation, decomposition, and destruction of HbA1c reach a steady state with about 3.0 percent to 6.5 percent of the hemoglobin being the A1c subtype. Most diabetic individuals have a higher HbA1c level. The actual HbA1c level can be used as an indicator of the average recent blood glucose level. This in turn indicates the possible level of glycation damage to tissues and thus of diabetic complications, if continued for years. And this, therefore, is why the HbA1c levels of diabetics need to be controlled.

Notice that the intervention described above did not rely on medications that are costly to health care systems, but rather the intervention relied on health education for secondary prevention to minimize the negative outcomes of diabetes. Weight reductions, HbA1c reductions, fewer daily medications, and fewer expensive emergency and hospital services are exceptional outcomes for a health care system that has its foundation in prevention and has very few resources to spend on preventable medical care.

Nevertheless, the treatment of DM in Cuba may be disturbing to some health care providers. Patient education is complex, and patient compliance is often problematic. At the same time, health care providers have not kept up with recent findings and are sometimes not skilled at diagnosis and treatment (Chin et al. 2000). A recent probability survey of 225 diabetics aged fifteen and older in the neighborhood of Diez de Octubre in Havana has clarified

DM patient perceptions about their DM care (Aldana Padilla et al. 1997). Some 87 percent of the respondents reported visiting their family physician office on a regular basis, 83 percent reported being satisfied with their health services, and 68 percent received courses of instruction of self-management (and 10 percent of these were from the family physician/nurse team, the rest by education specialists). At the same time, 15 percent expressed difficulty in getting attention for their disease, 68 percent said they were never examined with an ophthalmoscope for visual complications, 56 percent reported never having an examination of their feet, and only 43 percent had received the results of their glucose tests. As Aldana Padilla and co-authors concluded, the national program for diabetes care is not yet optimal.

OLDER PEOPLE: THE THIRD AGE

With the successes in reducing infant and maternal mortality and in establishing a countrywide primary health care network described previously, comes a benefit—increased life expectancy—that simultaneously presents the next major challenge for Cuba. Providing skilled care to the growing number of older Cubans who are most likely to have the multiple chronic diseases of the cardiovascular system and who become frail in their later years is the resultant challenge.

The 1995 National Survey of Risk Factors and Preventive Actions for Non-communicable Diseases gathered data on lifestyle and noncommunicable diseases among Cubans over 60. The survey reported that almost 69 percent of older people suffer from hypertension, including both the already diagnosed plus newly reported cases. Hypertension is the most frequent chronic disease among older people, followed by diabetes mellitus and ischemic heart disease. Some 51 percent reported a sedentary lifestyle, and among older people, there was a greater tendency toward being overweight than underweight (Martinez et al. 2000).

Cancer is the second leading cause of death in older Cubans, with this risk increasing with age until approximately eighty years old. In people over eighty, however, cancer causes a comparatively smaller number of deaths than in younger age groups. Overall, the death rate by age for neoplasms (cancers) has increased from 30 percent to 50 percent in men since 1950, but has declined 10 percent in women. In Cuba, the death rates in people over sixty for malignant tumors were 775 in 1995 and 799 in 1996 (per 100,000 inhabitants) (Oficina Nacional de Estadísticas, Centro de Estudios de Población y Desarrollo 1998). Regarding daily activities, the 1985 National Survey of Persons 60 and Over in Cuba revealed that the activities elders reported having difficulty carrying out on their own include going places far from home and climbing stairs (only 76 percent could perform these activities on their own). Over 93 percent of older people surveyed reported that they were able to carry out a series of activities on their own, which permitted them to remain at home alone eight to ten hours a day: eating their meals (if prepared in advance), taking their medicines, getting dressed, bathing, or going to the toilet in time.

In 2000, the Ministry of Health had declared four priorities for the future: (1) to continue the vast array of maternal and child health services, (2) to maintain their control over infectious diseases, (3) to begin to manage chronic diseases, and (4) to expand and improve care for seniors (Vega García 2000). The current services available for seniors include community senior centers, adult day treatment and care centers, home delivered meal programs, and supportive/assisted living. However, the supply and quality of these various services is neither extensive nor uniform throughout Cuba. The rural areas in particular appear underserved (Vega García 2000).

Cuba's vision for the future of its elders focuses on healthy longevity. Cuban health officials recognize that they will have to take a developmental prospective (e.g., it is important to start the control of osteoporosis earlier than age sixty). Cuban health officials also want an age-friendly society, including transportation systems and occupational safety programs that are recognized as prerequisites for healthy longevity. In Cuba as well as the United States, there is a painful recognition that the services available for today's frail elders are not adequate.

Having reviewed the Cuban experience with preventable diseases and the history of PHC in the Cuba public health system, we now turn to the larger epistemological question of how the "public" has come to be conceptualized in public health in recent years.

7

Recasting the "Public" in Public Health

Assessing the Cuban Experience

WHAT IS PUBLIC HEALTH?

We believe the Cuban Public Health Care (PHC) model demonstrates how increased equity, political will, and social capital synergistically combined to improve the health for all Cubans between 1959 and 2000. We also recognize that these improvements came with costs, that very real trade-offs between individualism and the public's common good were required to make those changes happen. In this chapter we ask a series of questions designed to contribute to the ongoing debate inside public health about the role of public health programs. We ask, for instance, What is the role of the "public" in public health, and how can the public participate in the provision of public health? The Cuban PHC model clearly relies on extensive community-based participation, be it in health promotion, vector eradication, compliance with vaccination campaigns, or neighborhood cleanup. Would such levels of participation be possible without coercion? Or without a history of mandatory neighborhood political organizations? Would PHC be possible without the Cuban levels of community-based participation? As we have also seen in the Cuban example, the state has far-reaching rights that can be used to intercede on behalf of the government-determined perception of the common good. Sometimes that intercession may result in the abrogation of individual rights, for instance, of whether or not to be inoculated or have blood screened.

How much responsibility does the state have to provide for the public's health? Is it, for instance, enough for the state to provide potable water and sewerage or must the government also protect the populace from the spread of infectious diseases? These are questions being asked by international public health researchers worldwide. Into this reconsideration of public health, questions about equity, empowerment, and equality are currently being considered as critical to the public health discussion. If equity and/or equality shape health outcomes, how does it work and how much must be present?

The answers to these questions are central to current health policy reforms, and epitomize the thorny issue of individual rights and state power. For the last one hundred years, the balance between the role of the government and the rights of individuals has shifted in the struggle to achieve and maintain public health. In many ways it is similar to the tensions between the role of government and the rights of individuals in the area of national security that have spread around the world in the twenty-first century. Finding that balance for health reform in any country is shaped by the national political, social, and ideological systems and also by the ability and desire of the populace to participate actively in the process of governance.

Regardless of development models, by the end of the twentieth century the disparities between rich and poor nations were not decreasing but rather were increasing. Similarity, the relative as well as absolute disparity within countries increased during the second half of the century (Wagstaff 2002; Wilkerson 1992; Wilkerson and Marmot 1998, 2003). By the late 1990s, health care reforms had moved away from comprehensive care models toward targeted or selective care, with the power situated outside of governmental agencies and in the hands of nongovernmental organizations (NGOs) or private, commercial health agencies (Janes 2004). The roles of both the public and the state in the provision of public health were diminished. By the end of the twentieth century, the great advances in public health from the preceding century and their concomitant public health infrastructures were in tatters. "Today's global health crisis reflects widening inequalities within and between countries. As the rich get richer and the poor get poorer, advances in science and technology are securing better health and longer lives for a small fraction of the world's population. Meanwhile, children die of diarrhea for want of clean water, people with AIDS die for want of affordable medicines, and poor people in all regions are increasingly cut off from the political, social, and economic tools they can use to create their own health and well-being" (Global Health Watch 2005:i).

While the Cuban PHC model may not be easily exportable, there are still many lessons that we can learn from it. Cuba provides an example of how relative equity (as measured by a relatively limited range of differences in income, access to education, employment, and health care) can maintain and support an effective public health system (UNPD 1999). Reductions in inequality appear to translate into better health outcomes, and conversely, societies with the greatest inequalities have overall poor health outcomes (Wilkerson 1992, 1996). In Cuba, access to those state supported resources is free and available to all Cubans regardless of ethnicity, gender, or income. This is not to say that there are no differences in levels of income, access to resources, or prejudice, but only that the *relative* differences within the population are not as great as before the Revolution or as common as in other countries throughout the Caribbean and South America. As we have seen in the case of Cuba, primary health care can function as an instrument of both the public and the state, where power is weighted in favor of the state. The state, in turns, uses that power to achieve traditional public health goals of reducing infectious disease, improving child and maternal health, and increasing longevity. The Cuban model, however, is also heavily dependent on the effective and ongoing involvement of local communities, involvement made possible by the achievements in reducing disparities in education, income, employment, and access to resources—and, some would argue, made necessary by the economic hardships imposed during the special period following the breakup of the Soviet Union when Cubans increasingly were asked to take on greater individual responsibility for their own health. That transfer of some personal health responsibilities is highlighted by the roles of neighborhood organizations to enforce that transfer.

At the beginning of this book, we noted that contradictions seem to underlie many aspects of Cuban life, including health care. The contradictions never seem more clear than in the health arena: the profusion of jineterismo in the midst of an effective HIV/AIDS prevention and control program; a "highly successful and respected" HIV/AIDS policy that is also hated and derided for human rights violations; high rates of smoking and throat and mouth cancer simultaneous with effective public health education to prevent lifestyle diseases.

However, Cuba is not alone in the paradoxes expressed between the public and the state—especially in "public" health. More than once in the history of organized public health institutions it has been asserted that public health is not, and has never been, about the health needs of the public, but rather it is about the ability of the government to provide a public infrastructure to safeguard health conditions and protect against epidemics to protect its labor force. In 1988, the Institute of Medicine (IOM) defined the mission of public as to fulfill society's interest in providing conditions in which people can be healthy (IOM 1988). And yet, many believe that now more than ever before, the state has obligations not just to provide a public health infrastructure to guard against epidemics but also to facilitate the reduction of social disparities and inequities that underlie cleavages in the health status of the public (Navarro and Shi 2001; Sachs and the Commission on Macroeconomics and Health 2001; Wagstaff 2002; Whiteford 2005). To use Farmer's term, the "structural violence" that reproduces social inequities shapes health outcomes (2004). Those who have resources may buy health; those who have not, do without.

The level of inequality existing today is made poignant when one recognizes that to provide and maintain "universal access to basic education, basic health care, adequate food, and safe water and sanitation for all has been estimated at less than 4 percent of the combined wealth of the 224 richest people in the world" (Global Health Watch 2005:2). According to the authors of Global Health Watch, equity and sustainability are the two major challenges pivotal in the struggle for public health, both in the last century and in the new millennium (2005:40). What the Cuban model shows is that in a society with reduced levels of both relative and absolute inequality, PHC can *produce* and *maintain* remarkable positive health outcomes.

Many people see a need for health reform and a reevaluation of state-run public health systems. However, there is no shared sense of what public health should be nor how it should be achieved. The conceptual schisms concerning how to envision public health and the government's responsibilities have increased as biotechnology and globalization converge in this arena. As Laurie Garrett notes in her book, *Betrayal of Trust: The Collapse of Global Public Health*, "The new century finds experts at odds over the mission of public health. No two deans of the West's major schools of public health agree on a definition of its goals and missions. While one school, the University of California, Berkeley, selected a biotechnology executive in 1998 as its dean, another, Harvard, opted that year for a leader whose battle was against the most ancient—even traditional—scourge, tuberculosis. A schism appeared and widened in academia, pitting technologists and health managers against the more traditional advocates of disease prevention and epidemiology" (2000:7). This division extends far beyond the selection of leaders of academic institutions entrusted to provide public health; it reflects the different paradigms expressed in global health initiatives.

In this quandary of public health, lessons can be learned from the process that created the epidemiological changes in the United Kingdom and the United States since the 1800s, which gave rise to modern public health. Those changes were made possible not through the development of biotechnology (the development of vaccines and antibiotics) but rather by the changed role of the state and political ideology (Szreter 1997). In a powerful article entitled "Economic Growth, Disruption, Deprivation, Disease, and Death: On the Importance of the Politics of Public Health for Development," Szreter convincingly demonstrates that changed political and social will were responsible for reductions in disease and improvements in mortality and morbidity rates in late nineteenth-century Britain. Szreter writes that as "economic growth translated into positive economic and social development when the relations of social capital in Britain's industrial communities were sufficiently strong that the politics of public health could *direct collective resources toward the good of the community as a whole*" (emphasis added) (1997:721). Potable water systems, urban sewerage systems, improved nutrition, and decent housing along with swamp drainage, river control measures, access to public education, and prenatal and maternal health care were instituted as public health practices. And when coupled with changes in political ideology, these initiatives resulted in significant and sustained improvement in the health of the British and American publics.

Szreter parses out the relationship between economic growth and development and argues that contrary to earlier opinions that economic growth results in development, economic growth may instead result in social and political disruptions, produce fomentation in extant ideologies and renegotiations of cultural and social values. Using documentation from Britain in the latter part of the nineteenth century, Szreter shows how equitable and comprehensive water and sanitation systems, which underlay the health improvements, were themselves a result of combined political and ideological changes toward providing for the common good of all, not just for those who could afford it. In short, health improvements resulted from increased equity in the provision of basic public health services for all, not just "targeted" improvements for those who could afford them.

Szreter's conclusions are important as we consider current models of public health and their underlying assumptions. One model, espoused by the Bill and Melinda Gates Foundation initiative, has disease- (or population-) targeted foci—for instance, HIV/AIDS, tuberculosis, and malaria—and is biotechnology-dependent. In contrast stands the model found in Cuba that is comprehensive, equity driven, low technology, and human resource dependent. The rise of non-governmental organizations, private foundations, and global public private initiatives (GPPIs), most of which focus on targeted interventions and are linked to a single disease, is shaped by the ideology of their founders and the organizations that fund them, regardless of the socio-political ideology of the governments in whose countries they provide services. The 2005 Global Health Watch reports that while WHO and UNICEF are significant actors, the World Bank and the Rockefeller and Gates Foundations, as well as some for-profit pharmaceutical companies are critical in policy decision making and financial allocations to health intervention programs. The authors of the report point out that certain groups are systematically excluded and the governmental and civil society organization of poor countries are virtually ignored. This disenfranchisement allows for the concentration of power in "multilateral institutions and the commercial sector" that often excludes governmental public health infrastructures (2005:74). This undermines the role of the state and local participatory community organizations.

Histories of corruption and misallocation of funds at national and local governmental levels encourages the creation of a parallel, non-governmental infrastructure. But that parallel NGO structure is often short-term and unaccountable to local people and their values.

MILLENNIUM GOALS AND CUBAN POLICY HISTORY

The effort to redefine health interventions and to recast public health is reflected in the UN Millennium Project (2005). In September 2000, leaders of 189 countries adopted the United Nations' Millennium Development Goals (MDGs) to improve the quality of life by 2015, with the ultimate aim of the project to end poverty. The United Nations Millennium Project identified eight development goals that established clear targets for "reducing poverty, hunger, disease, illiteracy, environmental degradation, and discrimination against women by 2015" (UN Millennium Project 2005).

The goals are to (1) eradicate extreme poverty and hunger; (2) achieve universal primary education; (3) promote gender equality and empower women; (4) reduce child mortality; (5) improve maternal health; (6) combat HIV/AIDS, malaria, and other diseases; (7) ensure environmental sustainability; and (8) develop a global partnership for development.

In order to know if these goals are being achieved before their 2015 deadline, a series of targets and indicators were established with data being collected by individual countries and stored in central MDG databases.

The MDG effort could be strengthened by learning from the seven principles that underlie the Cuban health system. As the documentation on Cuba shows, in the last 40 years, Cuba has successfully (1) reduced extreme hunger and poverty; (2) achieved universal primary education; (3) promoted gender equality and empowered women; (4) reduced child mortality; (5) improved maternal health; and is (6) combating HIV/AIDS, malaria, and other diseases; and (7) developing strategies for environmental sustainability utilizing multiple global partnerships for development (Waitzken et al. 1997; Zipperer 2005; Burr 1997; Hansen and Groce 2003; Farmer and Castro 2004). Integral elements of the United Nations' Declaration of the MDGs are the reduction of health disparities, the right of people to participate in the planning of their own health care, and the responsibility of governments to provide adequate and accessible health care to their citizens.

Just as the Declaration of Alma-Ata has had both immediate and long-term consequences, the United Nations' Millennium Project (of which the development goals are specific measures) holds the potential to shape global health policies and practices. Whether the Millennium Project goals will ever be achieved is not the point. Identifying these global goals and targeted milestones not only shapes policy but also forces the collection of data in these often overlooked or hidden areas. The importance of creating databases of country-specific health and environment data, identifying targeted goals for development, and providing means to measure progress toward the achievement of those goals *is* the point, and its importance cannot be underestimated. Data collection and publication are not small accomplishments, particularly for countries unaccustomed to the collection of epidemiology and social demographic data. So even if the MDG are not achieved by their targeted date of 2015, their very articulation combined with means of measurement will direct the future parameters of health policy from the national to the global stage.

The Millennium Development Goals were the result of ten task forces. Of particular interest here are the task forces directed toward Child and Maternal Health (Task Force 4) and the task force for HIV/AIDS, Malaria, TB, Other Major Diseases, and Access to Essential Medicines (Task Force 5). Each task force is made up of scholars and researchers, representatives of the public and private sector, and UN agencies. Their role is to help identify operational priorities, organizational means of implementation, and financing structures necessary to achieve identified goals.

Simultaneous to the development of the UN's Millennium Project, meeting of the WHO's Executive Board in 2000 proposed a review of the history and applications of PHC as well as its challenges in the changing context of global health. Health problems confronting the world are truly global in scale but require building blocks at the national level. Given the data accumulated about the Cuban PHC model and its health outcomes, it seems to be one model for the interlocking health promotion and disease prevention measures that could facilitate the achievement of some of the Millennium goals.

The MDGs are both impressive and offer an opportunity for global attention to identified public health problems. Designed to reduce global poverty, the Millennium Project, combined with the Report of the Commission on Macroeconomics and Health (Sachs and the Commission on Macroeconomics and Health 2001) draws attention to the need to link development and health explicitly, particularly as power and wealth appear to be increasingly consolidated in this new century. These two documents call for extensive new financial infusions and developments in health care. For this reason if for no other reason, they demand our attention.

By studying the Cuban PHC model, it could be possible to acquire important insights into how the MDGs could be achieved. It is not, however, suggested that the Cuban PHC is easily transferable nor that it necessarily should be. However, there are important lessons to be learned from the Cuban experience. It is time to reassert the primacy of equitable development to health, and sustained health to development as the *World Development Report: Investing in Health,* did twelve years ago (World Bank 1993; Whiteford 2005). This is particularly important in an era of increased belief in user fees and other profit-driven health policies in a period of neo-liberal trade reforms (Janes 2004). Sadly enough, there are no good data that demonstrate that these same neo-liberal reforms successfully reduce health disparities, let alone increase health equality. Continuing to replicate these models without that documentation is a failure of trust.

There are six MDGs that include health-related goals adapted from the World Health Organization (WHO) (Kekki 2003). To achieve the targeted goals of the remaining MDGs, policies and practices must be instituted to remediate the losses due to chronic and lifestyle-related diseases such as diabetes, heart disease, and stroke as well as addressing health disparities. The writers of the Millennium Projects and creators of the MDGs recognized that good health is critical to sustained economic development and the reduction of poverty. That recognition is clear in that three of the first seven MDGs are related to health; nine of the eighteen targets address health, and eighteen of the forty-eight indicators include health.

It is worth noting that one of the great achievements of the Cuban PHC model has been the successful reduction in health disparities. In Cuba, health benefits are distributed across the population and throughout the island. As noted earlier, even before the Revolution, Cuba had a better medical system than many other parts of the Caribbean, but it was concentrated in the capital and to a lesser extent in other cities, with little health care available in the countryside. This pattern is common in much of the developing world today. Following the Revolution, PHC in Cuba instituted island-wide equitable health access and universal public health promotion and education (Gomez 1999).

Because the MDGs build on specific and vertical programs rather than on universal and horizontal programs for health improvements, one fear is that the MDGs may result in improvements but only in targeted areas rather than for all. Horizontal programs, like the Cuban PHC model, focus on universal and free access based on principles of social justice delivered equally to the poor or marginalized parts of the population. The effect then is to reduce disparities resulting from a history of exclusion and neglect by offering special programs to populations previously excluded (equity).

Such a model would emphasize organization, coverage, quality, effectiveness, performance, human resources, capacity building, social participation, and accountability—factors emphasized by the WHO report as necessary conditions for maximizing the health of populations. Some other aspects central to PHC such as the treatment of non-communicable chronic diseases, human resources, and health systems organization are not specifically covered by the MDGs. Nonetheless, they are critical to improving standards of health for all people rather than for just identified subgroups.

While the MDGs are useful heuristics, the documents do not say how to achieve these goals. The Global Health Watch 2005–2006, however, does lay out an agenda to reassert the principles of Alma-Ata and PHC. It suggests that the best strategy would be to strengthen the public sector and to establish mechanisms for governmental accountability in health care (2005:83–95). Its framework is based on equity and participation as critical building blocks for health care reform.

We conclude this chapter by revisiting the concept of "equity" and its role in health reform. An "equity lens" is important because political and economic institutions are shaped in ways that can reinforce unfair advantages and widen socioeconomic disparities. The conditionalities imposed upon poor governments by the World Bank and International Monetary Fund (IMF) are undemocratic and have included the privatization of public assets, thereby undermining public education and health care systems and eroding social safety nets (Global Health Watch 2005:4). Without a publicly supported public health system, equity will be difficult to achieve and impossible to maintain.

In this book, we have used the concept of equity as Wilkerson (1992), Wilkerson and Marmot (2003), Farmer (2004) do. That means not only equality but more importantly that those most in need receive attention first, and then assistance to the rest. The provision of universal access to education and health care are two central means to reduce inequities and inequalities. In combination with effective local participation, the three provide the base to reduce the consequences of structural violence too often visited upon the marginalized, poor, and powerless.

Returning to the lessons learned from the epidemiological transition of Britain and the United States during the nineteenth century, we concur that the "silver bullet" theory of vertical health programs is inadequate, and it is time for what Nathanson (1996), Bambra and colleagues (2005), and others have proposed as a theory of public health based on socio-political, ideological, and participatory frameworks to achieve equity. To return the "public" to health care there must be an educated, informed, and healthy public with a tradition of participation in their health care decisions. In addition, public health cannot be thought of, as Laurie Garrett wrote is the case in the United States, as "just health care for the poor" (2000) but rather health care for all. By applying the lessons learned from the analysis of the social and political changes that made possible the public health successes of the twentieth century, we can learn from the successes in this century of the Cuban PHC model.

8

Lessons Learned from Cuba's Primary Health Care Model

In this final chapter we distill what we have learned from our analysis of the Cuban Primary Health Care (PHC) experience into ten lessons. We recognize that the Cuban situation is unique in many aspects: its enduring authoritarian political system, the longevity of its president, the sustained political will supporting health and equity, the relative lack of mobility of the populace, that it is a small island country, and the Cuban culture itself. We also recognize that there are many lessons those interested in health reform in specific and general public health can learn from this case. They can learn that equity really does facilitate health outcome improvements and that the reduction of disparities really does reflect significant changes in cultural practices and attitudes. They can learn that universal access does not have to reduce the quality of health services but rather can be associated with strengthening services. The Cuban case also exemplifies how community-based care and effective community participation synergistically strengthen one another and how health promotion can lead to behavioral and lifestyle changes.

Spatial and temporal variables also influence the successes from the Cuban case. There are about eleven million people living in Cuba, and with little immigration or emigration they are a relatively stable population. Most PHC physicians live in their own catchment areas, stay there for a prolonged period, and the families they treat remain in the neighborhood as well. This creates a situation not found in many other countries. The relative lack of mobility, just as the continuity provided by the enduring political leadership and its commitment to public and political health policies and programs, makes Cuba an unusual case. The political will, local community participation, and increased equity combine to mutually reinforce the constant underlying and explicit theme that "prevention works."

109

Other lessons offered from the Cuban case are that Cuba's relative size and isolation may work for it and cases in both size and international connectedness might mitigate some of its successes (Whiteford and Hill 2005). And, finally, even in the Cuban case, not everything works as well as one would wish. The Cuban preventive health model is effective, community-based, and relatively technology independent. And even then, many health posts do not have access to even the most basic of medicines (Waitzkin et al. 1997). Curative care is not the same as preventative care and is much more problematic.

As we discuss the lessons, we hope the reader imagines how these lessons might be applied elsewhere. Since the 1960s, many countries (as well as Cuba) have incorporated a rural *pasantía* (residency) as part of the training of physicians. However, in too many of those countries it has been a less than successful experience (Whiteford 1990), so it is not the rural experience itself that marks the Cuban experience but rather the continuity of community-based care on which the PHC model is based. "What makes the Cuban system unique is the manner in which the delivery of care has been fused with public health. Cuban family physicians are trained to focus, in epidemiological terms, on the overall health of the people they serve. They provide the best possible care for a patient who comes through the door of their clinic with symptoms of diabetes, but they put just as much emphasis on preventing the onset of diabetes in their community and the early detection of cases" (London School of Economics 2003:1). The successful rural *pasantía* experience and the Cuban emphasis on community-based health prevention contribute to the model's ability to be generalized. A physician interviewed by Lemkau told her: "All physicians should have to serve in the countryside. Medical school taught me about medicine, but the mountains taught me about community. The community is the center of my life" (Lemkau 2004).

Perhaps that which most distinguishes Cuba from countries that could benefit from its PHC model is the civil will and symbolic capital that Cuba has developed in the decades since the Revolution. Feinsilver (2002), Whiteford (2000), and Castro and Farmer (2004) have each identified the role that symbolic capital plays in developing and maintaining the Cuban PHC model, each attributing part of the model's success to the role that local communities and civil groups as well as to the national government played in the model's development and maintenance. The reduction in class differences, the provision of free education, the improvement of the life of the poor, and the provision of "health for all" succeed in fostering a sense of equality not found in many places.

We are not, however, arguing that these improvements came without costs, or that they resulted in a perfect system. We are suggesting that the changes resulted in a more *equitable* system that reduced disparities among sectors of the population. In so doing, it realigned the forces responsible for maintaining the structural violence that consistently privileged the wealthy, urban, white, professional class to the detriment of the less educated, darker, rural members of the population.

We recognize the many ways that the Cuban PHC model reflects the uniquely Cuban experience; we also acknowledge that there are significant lessons to be drawn from the almost fifty years of developing the Cuban PHC model. Cuba's success in achieving well-documented increased equity within the populace, radical reduction in extreme poverty and hunger, significant improvements in child and maternal health, impressive eradication and control of infectious and contagious diseases, environmental surveillance and protection programs, and collaborative partnerships—particularly with members of the European Union—make its model worth serious and careful attention.

A recent publication from the World Health Organization (WHO) adds the concept of "empowerment" as effectively underlying health improvements (WHO 2006). "Within the last decades, social exclusion, disparities, and absolute poverty—almost three billion people living on less than $2.00 USD per day—have grown despite globalization and rising per capita income in many developing nations. Worldwide health disparities are increasing due to vulnerability to disease from severe malnutrition, rapid re-emergence of water and blood-borne infectious diseases, environment degradation, disinvestment in the health infrastructure and violence. Within the same period, empowerment strategies, participation, and other bottom-up approaches have become prominent paradigms within public health and the development aid for reducing these disparities" (WHO 2006:4). While not a bottom-up design, the Cuban PHC model effectively demonstrates one case of health care empowerment and its associated health outcome successes. With these ideas in mind, we turn to the lessons learned from the Cuban experience.

LESSON ONE: REDUCTION OF DISPARITIES

The first and most global lesson to be learned from the Cuban experiment is the importance of reducing disparities in health outcomes, access, opportunities, education, and access to resources. By reducing—not necessarily removing but by drastically reducing—both the relative and absolute differences within the population, the overall indicators of well being improve. Wilkerson's (1996) provocative ideas about the physical as well as social damage accrued in settings of relative differences in access to resources, class, education, and occupation appear to be borne out in Cuba (Chomsky 2000:331-357). By reducing these disparities in relative as well as absolute terms, Cuba acquired considerable social and symbolic capital, health empowerment, as well as good health in its own society. "The health outcomes in those who live in inegalitarian societies are inferior to those who live in more egalitarian societies [and have] led to the observations that some societies are, indeed, 'unhealthy'" (Nguyen and Peschard 2003:450). The value of social capital and civil or good will generated by sustained and successful attempts to reduce social, educational, and economic disparities should not be underestimated. In a country of shortages such as Cuba as well as in many other developing countries, the acknowledgment of reduced disparities matters.

LESSON TWO: HEALTH FOR ALL

Even critics of the Cuban health care system recognize that access to health care across the island is remarkable. "Indeed, there is a strong medical presence everywhere in Cuba. In Alamar, a community northeast of the city of Havana, a polyclinic was staffed with two physicians and three nurses on a quiet Sunday afternoon. In close proximity, there were family physician residences in the neighborhood. In Miramar, on the western side of the city, a child care center with 320 children has one physician and three nurses on its regular staff. There was a physician and a nurse in the Jose Diaz Colina cigar factory with about 580 workers. A sugar cane cooperative outside of Havana has 126 members and a visiting physician and nurse. Havana Psychiatric Hospital, with 4,000 beds and 3,400 patients, has 100 physicians, including 20 psychiatrists, as well as 2,000 employees including other health-related professionals" (Nayeri 1995).

LESSON THREE:
HEALTH CARE IN AND OF THE COMMUNITY

Accessibility and reliability are critical elements in developing and maintaining trust between health care providers and the people they serve. Having community-based health care means that health posts, polyclinics, and family physicians are never too far away in Cuba. This model works because of the emphasis on not only locating clinics in communities, but also training family medicine physicians to staff them. This is easier to do when people have restricted choices as they do in Cuba (for both the physicians and the community), thereby guaranteeing the training and staffing required. Even then, as Crabb (2001) and others have pointed out, simply having clinics, nurses, and physicians is not enough where there are no supplies. Clearly, the model of family medicine in the community requires sufficient support to make it work well.

LESSON FOUR:
EFFECTIVE COMMUNITY PARTICIPATION

The Cuban PHC model situates the basic building blocks of the health care system within the community. Simultaneously it places some of the responsibility for the system within the community. This obligation is shared between the government and the public, each with its own responsibilities and obligations. Cuba has been able to build effectively on extant community-based organizations and groups. Many of these groups—the Committee for the Defense of the Revolution (CDR) and the Federation of Cuban Women, for instance—were originally designed to further the causes of the Revolution by keeping close track of people's activities. This very supervision, combined with the aims of the Revolution being furthered through improved health, formed a powerful tool for community participation. In contrast to other Caribbean and Latin American countries where community participation campaigns failed, in Cuba, community participation is a critical and respected portion of the model (Heggenhougen 1993; Whiteford 1997). In contrast to other health care models, assessments of the Cuban health care model require and respond to public opinion and community evaluations. Theodore Macdonald, professor of health promotion at Brunel University in London, suggests that in Cuba, neighborhood empowerment is successfully transformed into implementation of social policy (Anonymous 1991). In part this occurs through the existence and empowerment of community groups and also through the shared gathering of information pertinent to their operation. Neighborhood health units collect health information that is shared with the government, and the government trains them to analyze data and participate in health promotion campaigns.

LESSON FIVE: HEALTH PROMOTION

Throughout Cuba, billboards and posters exhort the populace to save water, wash their hands, cover their food, and avoid excesses. Given the relative absence of any non-political billboards, the health promotion messages are clear and frequent. Health promotion does not have to be expensive, but it does have to be consistent and sustained for maximum effectiveness. According to Greene (citing Macdonald), Cuba was one of the first countries to implement health promotion policies as part of its national goals (2003:107). Again according to Macdonald, "One explanation for Cuba's advances in health promotion is that the policies depend strongly not primarily on the sorts of pharmacologically and clinically centered interventions, but on broad social awareness of the link of social factors, lifestyles, and health" (Greene 2003:108).

LESSON SIX:
SUSTAINED COMMITMENT TO PHC FOR
PUBLIC HEALTH POLICIES

Health policy in Cuba is the result of a prolonged and sustained commitment to improving health for all its populace. That commitment has been led and maintained by Fidel Castro for almost fifty years. Few other governments have combined long-term and almost absolute power centered in one individual with an unflagging commitment to health improvements. In far too many other governments, health policy is rarely a priority, and if so, is not sustained. Too often, public health is not taken to mean what John Duffy suggests it should be: public health "means—and always has meant—community action to avoid disease and other threats to the health and welfare of individuals at large" (Duffy 1990:2, cited in Nathanson 1996:631). Community action—the responsibility and obligations of the community—can succeed only with the political and economic support of the government; neither operates in isolation to improve and maintain public health. Indeed, the Cuban case study exemplifies the points made by Nathanson in her 1996 article "Disease Prevention as Social Change: Toward a Theory of Public Health." In that article Nathanson posits: "(1) that public health policies play a critical role in disease prevention and in the decline of mortality; (2) that the formulation, adoption, and implementation of these policies are the outcome of social and political processes; and (3) that sufficient knowledge currently exists to identify these processes and to articulate them in the form of researchable hypotheses" (1996: 609–610).

LESSON SEVEN:
PREVENTION WORKS

First and foremost, the Cuban PHC model has demonstrated on several different levels that a commitment to disease prevention can be successful. Infectious communicable diseases are traditionally the scourges of developing and poor countries. Without waiting to become developed and rich, Cuba has demonstrated that it is possible for a developing country to eradicate malaria (1959–1967), poliomyelitis (1959–1994), and diphtheria (1962–1970), providing a blueprint for other developing countries to adapt and implement in their own contexts.

Cuba has demonstrated that health promotion campaigns can be implemented successfully. One case in point is the extensive prenatal and postnatal care programs that have resulted in lowering the infant mortality rate in Cuba to levels well below that achieved in the United States.

LESSON EIGHT: SIZE MAY MATTER

Cuba's success in disease prevention and health promotion campaigns may be attributable in part to the relatively small size of the island nation. The total population of Cuba is slightly more than eleven million people, with equal numbers of women and men. Cuba has fourteen provinces and one island municipality within its 44,213 square miles, and ranges from extreme urban density in its capital city of Havana with nearly 2.2 million inhabitants to extremely rural conditions in four of the provinces. For a comparison to a U.S. context, in the 2000 U.S. census the state of Ohio had 11.3 million people within its 41,222 square miles, essentially the same geographic area and the same population base as Cuba's. However, the long and narrow shape of Cuba is different from the square shape of Ohio, as evidenced by a journey of approximately 800 miles from the eastern tip of Cuba to the western tip, contrasted with a trip of slightly less than 300 miles between northeast and southwest Ohio. Notwithstanding the difference in travel mileage, the comparability of population size and square mileage transforms a discussion about a national health care system for Cuba equivalent to a discussion about a system that would meet the needs of a population the size of Ohio.

Achieving consensus is easier among smaller populations than among larger populations. Furthermore, forty-five years under the same national leadership in Cuba arguably makes consensus easier to achieve than in places with leadership changes every four to eight years. And lastly, policy consensus is easier to achieve in a socialistic dictatorship than in democracies, particularly democracies that emphasize individual rights compared to democracies that emphasize the common good.

LESSON NINE:
PREVENTIVE HEALTH CARE AND
CURATIVE MEDICINE ARE VERY DIFFERENT

Epidemiologic studies have identified specific risk factors that increase people's likelihood of contracting specific diseases. Some of the risk factors presently are amenable to change (e.g., lifestyle factors like diet, exercise, and smoking); others are not easily changeable at present (e.g., genetic or environmental). To effect behavioral change among the ameliorable risk factors through community interventions and individual counseling is the heart and soul of evidenced-based health promotion and disease prevention.

Community interventions and individual counseling are labor intensive and require skilled training, but most of the time, such health promotion and disease prevention activities are not capital intensive and do not require the financial resources that characterize so much of high-technology curative medicine in the developed countries during the twenty-first century.

LESSON TEN:
CURATIVE HEALTH CARE IS VERY EXPENSIVE

Curative medicine is extremely costly. The United States, for example, spent over $1.1 trillion dollars for personal health care in 2000 and continues to spend more per individual on health (over $4,000 per person) than any other country in the world (National Center for Health Statistics 2002). In 2003, the United States had 965,256 staffed beds in registered hospitals, or approximately 3.4 beds per 1,000 population (American Hospital Association 2004). In the United States the average charges for a day in an acute hospital—without any surgical charges—is approximately $1,400 (Kaiser Family Foundation n.d.). One can go into virtually any hospital in the United States and observe hospital rooms that exude a level of technology that can take one's breath away.

In contrast, Cuba reported a hospital bed rate of 5.2 per 1,000 population in 2000 (PAHO 1998:238), but an inspection of the hospitals demonstrates a lack of supplies and outdated technologies. Furthermore, the per capita income in Cuba is estimated at $2,000 USD a year. Comparing this $2,000 annual per capita income in Cuba with the $4,000 annual per capita health care costs in the United States and the $1,400 a day average cost of a non-surgical bed in a U.S. hospital, it is easy to see that Cuba does not have the economic resources to emphasize curative medicine as is done in the United States, nor is curative medicine necessarily a model to be emulated.

Given that Cuba's health care forte is prevention and that the United States' strength in health care is curative medicine with a reliance on high technology and pharmacology, it is legitimate to ask why both prevention and curative medicine cannot seem to coexist with equal emphasis. The complete answer to that question is yet to be found.

In the United States, with the latest technologies, highly trained, specialized staffs to use them, and the resources available to pay for the curative treatment of myocardial infarctions, cerebral hemorrhages, and a host of other preventable diseases, it is difficult to change the dominant paradigm from curative health care to preventive health care.

We have reported earlier that medical tourism is a growth industry in Cuba. To compete in the global industry of medical tourism, three things are required: (1) highly trained physicians, nurses, and other medical staff; (2) the most up-to-date diagnostic and treatment equipment (i.e., high technology medical supplies); and (3) pharmaceuticals. Apparently, Cuba's policies allow those three components to be directed to medical tourism, but they are often not available for the Cuban people themselves.

The success of the Cuban experience provides a model for other countries to achieve health improvements, even without significant increases in per capita income. As Szreter's detailed reevaluation of Thomas McKeown's work on mortality decline in nineteenth and early twentieth-century Britain demonstrates, while improved nutrition and standard of living are not inconsiderable in accounting for the mortality decline, "the role of a battling public health ideology, politics, and medicine operating of necessity through local government, is more correctly seen as the principal causal agency involved" (Szreter 1988:36). Szreter makes clear that he is not referring to technologically dependent medicine but rather to "organized human agency as represented by the public health movement" (Nathanson 1996:610) that accounts for the precipitous mortality decline. This is, we believe, what the Cuban model clearly demonstrates.

In this book we have presented the case of the Cuban PHC model within the context of the WHO's design to reduce poverty and improve human health and the UN's Millennium Project. We hope that readers will have learned about Cuba from this book but also that they will have learned how leadership, public policy, and community ownership can create a model to effectively reduce disparities, improve child and maternal health, and reduce infectious disease and how lessons learned from these efforts can be applied to other countries. We began writing the book with our interest in the apparent contradictions of the Cuban system: free and universal access to health and education in a political system with very few individual freedoms and an outstanding PHC model built on powerful and sustained community involvement, mandated by the government. Equity built on all having very little; successful eradication of infectious childhood diseases and clinics without basic supplies. Perhaps these contradictions may best be understood with reference to two terms used commonly in Cuba to explain everything: *la lucha* (to continue the struggle) and *resolver* (to overcome). We hope that Cuba may continue to "resolver" the problems it faces and that the rest of the world may continue to learn from Cuba to strive toward equity and health.

Bibliography

Aldana Padilla, Deysi, Irina Hernández Cuesta, Ileana Allison Megret, and René Guarnaluse Arce. 1997. Evaluación de la atención al paciente diabético en un área de salud. *Revista Cubana Salud Pública* 23 (1–2): 78–87.

Alonso, José F., Ricardo A. Donate-Armada, and Armando M. Lago. 1994. A first approximation design of the social safety net for a democratic Cuba. *Cuba in Transition: Proceedings of the Fourth Annual Meeting of the Association for the Study of the Cuban Economy (ASCE), held at Florida International University, Miami, FL, on August 11–13, 1994*. Miami, Fla.: Association for the Study of the Cuban Economy (ASCE). http://lanic.utexas.edu/la/cb/cuba/asce/cuba4/healsys1.html (accessed July 29, 2005).

Álvarez Li, Frank Carlos. 1998. Epidemiología de la enfermedad cerebrovascular en Cuba. *Primero Congreso Virtual Ibero-americano de Neurología*. Congreso Virtual Ibero-americano de Neurología. http://neurologia.rediris.es/congreso-1/conferencias/epidemiol-5-1.html (accessed July 29, 2005).

American Cancer Society. 2005. Cigarette smoking. www.cancer.org/docroot/PED/content/PED_10_2X_Cigarette_Smoking.asp?sitearea=PED (accessed July 29, 2005).

American Hospital Association. 2004. Fast facts on U.S. hospitals from AHA hospital statistics. www.aha.org/aha/resource_center/fastfacts/fast_facts_US_hospitals .html (accessed July 29, 2005).

Anderson, Robert N. 2002. Division of Vital Statistics, *CDC national vital statistics report: Deaths: Leading causes for 2000*, volume 50, number 16.

Anonymous. 1991. Flyer for Theodore Macdonald lecture at the London School of Economics.

Bambra, Claire, Debbie Fox, and Alex Scott-Samuel. 2005. Towards a politics of health. *Health Promotion International* 20 (2): 187–94.

Barberia, Lorena, Arachu Castro, and Dan Nemser. eds. 2002. *Seminar on Cuban health system: its evolution, accomplishments and challenges*. Working Papers on Latin

America, 02/03–4. Cambridge, Mass.: David Rockefeller Center for Latin American Studies.

Beldarraín Chapel, Enrique. n.d. "Historical Evolution of Epidemics Diseases in Cuba Until the End of the 20th Century." Unpublished document.

Bennett, Murphy S. 1999. *Psychology and Health Promotion.* Buckingham, UK: Open University Press.

Bentley, Molley. 2003. Cuba leads the way in HIV fight. *BBC News*, February 17. http://news.bbc.co.uk/1/hi/in_depth/sci_tech/2003/denver_2003/2770631.stm (accessed November 23, 2005).

Blane, D., E. Brunner, and R. Wilkerson, eds. 1996. *Health and Social Organization: Towards a Health Policy for the Twenty-first Century,* London: Routledge.

Bosetti, C., M. Malvezzi, E. Chatenoud, F. Levi, and C. La Vecchia. 2005. Trends in cancer mortality in the Americas, 1970–2000. *Annals of Oncology* 16: 489–511.

Branch, L. G., E. A. Borrayo, J. T. Sykes, E. V. Garcia. 2004. An introduction to the current Cuban health care system: The case of elder care. *Global Ageing* 2(2): 15–27.

Burr, Chandler. 1997. Assessing Cuba's approach to contain AIDS and HIV. *The Lancet* 350 (9078): 647.

Casal, Gloria, Antonio A. Fernández, Pedro Melchor González, and Pedro F. Pellet. 2002. Health care in Cuba and in the United States of America: An eclectic approach. *Cuba in Transition: papers and proceedings of the Twelfth Annual Meeting of the Association for the Study of the Cuban Economy (ASCE),* Coral Gables, August 3–5, 2002, 445–49. Coral Gables, Fla.: Association for the Study of the Cuban Economy (ASCE). http://lanic.utexas.edu/project/asce/pdfs/volume12/pellet.pdf (accessed August 2, 2005).

Castro, Arachu. 2002. Personal communication.

Castro, Arachu, and Paul Farmer. 2004. Health economics. In *Encyclopedia of Medical Anthropology: Health and Illness in the World's Cultures.* Edited by E.C. R. and M. Ember, vol. 1, Topics. New York: Kluwer Academic/Plenum Publishers.

Castro, Arachu, and Merrill Singer, eds. 2004. *Unhealthy Health Policy: A Critical Anthropological Examination.* Walnut Creek, Calif.: AltaMira Press.

Castro, Fidel. 1953. *History will absolve me.* Fidel Castro self-defense speech before the court in Santiago de Cuba on October 16, 1953. Radio Havana Cuba.

Centers for Disease Control and Prevention. 1993. Cigarette smoking—attributable mortality and years of potential life lost—United States, 1990. *Morbidity and Mortality Weekly Report* 42 (33): 645–49.

Central Intelligence Agency (CIA). 2005. *The World Factbook—Cuba.* www.cia.gov/ cia/publications/factbook/geos/cu.html (accessed November 23, 2005, and July 23, 2006).

Chin, Marshall H., et al. 2000. Quality of diabetes care in community health centers. *American Journal of Public Health.* 90 (3): 431–34.

Chin, M. H., et al. 2000. Quality of diabetes care in community health centers. *American Journal of Public Health.* 90 (3): 431–34.

Chomsky, Aviva. 2000. The threat of a good example: Health and revolution in Cuba. In *Dying For Growth: Global Inequality and the Health of the Poor.* Edited by J. Y. Kim, J. V. Miller, A. Irwin, and J. Gershman. 331–57. Monroe: Common Courage Press.

Crabb, Mary Catherine. 2001. "Socialism, Health and Medicine in Cuba: A Critical Re-Appraisal." Ph.D. diss., Emory University, Atlanta, Ga.

De Vos, Pol. 2005. 'No one left behind': Cuba's national health system since the 1959 revolution. *International Journal of Health Services*, vol. 35, no.1. 189–207.

Delgado Zapata, Silvia, Digna Valdespino Llerena, and Jesús Malpica Selleck. Enfermedades cerebrovasculares, investigación de los servicios y calidad del proceso de atención médica. Un Nuevo enfoque. 2000. *RESUMED*, 13 (4): 170–173.

Descriptive Epidemiology Group. 2005. Cancer Mondial International Agency for Research on Cancer (IARC). www-dep.iarc.fr.

La Dirección Nacional de Estadística del Ministerio de Salud Pública de Cuba. 1999.

Documento de la OPS. 1972. Los datos referidos en este epígrafe fueron tomados del *Informe para la Certificación y Registro de la Malaria en Cuba.* Diciembre de 1972.

Doll, Richard, and Richard Peto. 1981. *The Causes of Cancer. Quantitative Estimates of Avoidable Risks of Cancer in the United States Today.* New York: Oxford University Press.

Domínguez Álvarez, Joel, Alfredo Novales Amado, Ricardo Brañas Valdés, and Arturo Jesús Pérez Corrales. 1999. Mortalidad por enfermedades cerebrovasculares en mayores de 15 anos. *Revista Cubana De Medicina General Integral* 15 (3): 252–58.

Domínguez, Jorge I. 2002. Cuban health care: some political considerations. In *Seminar on Cuban health system: Its evolution, accomplishments and challenges December 11, 2001.* Edited by Lorena Barberia, Arachu Castro, and Dan Nemser. A33–A36. Cambridge, Mass.: David Rockefeller Center for Latin American Studies. www.medanthro.net/docs/castro_cuba.pdf.

Donaldson, Raymond J., and Liam J. Donaldson. 1994. *Essential Public Health Medicine.* Dordrecht; Boston: Kluwer Academic Publishers.

Donate-Armada, Ricardo A. 1994. Cuban social security: A preliminary actuarial analysis of law #24 of social security. *Proceedings of the Fourth Annual Meeting of the Association for the Study of the Cuban Economy (ASCE),* held at Florida International University, Miami, Fla., on August 11–13, 1994. http://lanic.utexas.edu/la/cb/cuba/asce/cuba4/donatear1.html (accessed February 9, 2006).

Doyal, Leslie, and Imogen Pennell. 1979. *The Political Economy of Health.* London: Pluto Press.

Duffy, John. 1990. *The Samaritans: A History of American Public Health.* Urbana and Chicago: University of Illinois Press.

The Economist. 2000. In the Shadows: Organized criminals run a thriving business smuggling women for the sex industry. What can be done to thwart them? August 24.

Farmer, Paul. 2004. *Pathologies of Power: Health, Human Rights and the New War on the Poor.* California Series in Public Anthropology, 4. Berkeley: University of California Press.

Farmer, Paul, and Arachu Castro. 2004. Pearls of the Antilles? Public health in Haiti and Cuba. In *Unhealthy Health Policy: A Critical Anthropological Examination.* Edited by Arachu Castro and Merrill Singer. Walnut Creek, Calif.: AltaMira Press.

Feinsilver, Julie Margot. 1989. Cuba as a "world medical power": The politics of symbolism. *Latin American Research Review* 24 (2):1–34.

———. 1993. *Healing the Masses: Cuban Health Politics at Home and Abroad.* Berkeley: University of California Press.

———. 2002. Three decades of health reform: 1960–1990. In *Seminar on Cuban health system: Its evolution, accomplishments and challenges December 11, 2001. Eds.*

Lorena Barberia, Arachu Castro, and Dan Nemser, A21–A25. Cambridge, Mass.: David Rockefeller Center for Latin American Studies. www.medanthro.net/docs/castro_cuba.pdf.

Fernández Concepción, Otman, Lenin Luna Rodríguez, Miguel A. Buergo Zuaznábar, and Miriam Concepción Rojas. 2002. Characterization of patients with cerebral infarcts discharged from a hospital in la Havana in 1998. *Revista De Neurología* 32 (10): 929–34. www.neurologia.com/VeureResum.asp?i=i&Ref=2000609&Par1=DeAutor.asp&Par2=32&Par3=10. (accessed July 29, 2005).

Galán Alvarez, Yaima H., M. E. Guerra Yi, Leticia M. Fernández Garrote, and R. Camacho Rodríguez. 2004. Incidence, mortality and survival from prostate cancer in Cuba, 1977–1999. *European Journal of Cancer Prevention* 3 (5): 377–81.

García, Rosario, and Rolando Suárez. 1996. Diabetes education in the elderly: A 5-year follow-up of an interactive approach. *Patient Education and Counseling* 29 (1): 87–97.

Garrett, Laurie. 2000. *Betrayal of Trust: The Collapse of Global Public Health.* 1st ed. New York: Hyperion.

Gilpin, Margaret. 1991. Update—Cuba: On the road to a family medicine nation. *Journal of Public Health Policy.* Spring: 83–103.

Global Health Watch. 2005. 2005/2006 Report. Global Health Watch. *Global Health Watch 2005–2006: An alternative world health report.* London: Zed. www.ghwatch.org/2005report/ghw.pdf. (accessed July 29, 2005).

Gómez, F. Cobarrubias. 1999. *Investigación sobre desarrollo humano y equidad en Cuba 1999.* Havana: United Nations.

Granich, R., B. Jacobs, J. Mermin, and A. Pont. 1995. Cuba's national AIDS program: The first decade. *The Western Journal of Medicine* 163 (2): 139–45.

Graupera Boschmonar, Margarita C., Pedro J. Jiménez Chaviano, Antonio A. Martín García, Yaima H. Galán Alvarez, Leticia M. Fernández Garrote, and R. Sankaranarayanan. 1999. Trends in survival rates of cancer in Cuba. *European Journal of Epidemiology* 15 (6): 521–28.

Greene, Ruby. 2003. Effective community health participation strategies: A Cuban example. *International Journal of Health Planning and Management* 18(2): 105–16.

Guillermoprieto, Alma. 2001. *Looking for History: Dispatches from Latin America.* New York: Pantheon Press.

Guillermoprieto, Alma. 2004. *Dancing with Cuba: A Memoir of the Revolution.* New York: Random House, Inc.

Guzman, Maria G., and Khouri, Gustavo. 2002. Dengue update. *The Lancet* 2:33–42.

Hansen, Helena, and Nora Groce. 2003. Human immunodeficiency virus and quarantine in Cuba. *Journal of the American Medical Association* 290 (12): 2875–75.

Heggenhougen, H. H. Kristian. 1984. Will primary health care efforts be allowed to succeed? *Social Science and Medicine* 19 (3): 217–24.

———. 1993. PHC and anthropology: challenges and opportunities. *Culture, Medicine and Psychiatry* 17: 281–89.

Hernández Cañero, Alberto. 1999. Mortality from ischemic heart disease in Cuba. The role of diet and serum cholesterol. *Revista Cubana de Cardiologia y Cirugia Cardiovascular* 13 (1): 8–12.

Holan, P., and Nelson Phillips. 1997. Sun, sand, and hard currency: Tourism in Cuba. *Annals of Tourism Research* 24 (4): 777–95.

Hsieh, Ying-Hena, Cathy W. Chen, Shen-Ming Lee, and Hector de Arazoza. 2001. On the recent sharp increase in HIV detections in Cuba. *AIDS* 15 (3): 426–28.

Iatridis, Demetrius. 1990. Cuba's health care policy: Prevention and active community participation. *Social Work* 35 (1): 29–35.

Institute of Medicine (IOM). 1988. Committee for the study of the future of public health. *The Future of Public Health.* Washington D.C.: National Academic Press.

Iyer, Pico. 2004. Elegiac carnival. In *Cuba: True Stories.* Edited by Tom Miller, 5–13. San Francisco, Calif.: Travelers' Tales.

Janes, Craig R. 2004. Going global in century XXI: Medical anthropology and the new primary health care. *Human Organization* 63 (4): 457–72.

Joly, O. G., J. H. Lubin, and M. Caraballose. 1983. Dark tobacco and lung cancer in Cuba. *Journal of the National Cancer Institute* 70 (6): 1033–39.

——. 1984. Dark tobacco and lung cancer in Cuba. *World Smoking Health* 9 (2): 21–26.

Justice, Judith. 1986. *Policies, Plans, and People: Foreign Aid and Health Development: Comparative Studies of Health Systems and Medical Care.* Berkeley: University of California.

Kaiser Family Foundation. n.d. Kaiser statehealthfacts.org. http://statehealthfacts.org (accessed July 29, 2005).

Kark, S.L., and E. Kark. 1983. An alternative strategy in community health care: community-oriented primary health care. *Israel Journal of Medical Science* 19(8):707–13.

Kawabata, Kei, Ke Xu Kei, and Guy Carrin. 2002. Preventing impoverishment through protection against catastrophic health expenditure. *Bull World Health Organization* 2002:612–15.

Kekki, Pertti. 2003. *Primary Health Care and the Millennium Development Goals: Issues for Discussion.* World Health Organization. The Global Meeting on Future Strategic Directions for Primary Health Care October 17–20. www.who.int/chronic_conditions/primary_health_care/en/mdgs_final.pdf.

Kemm J. and A. Close. 1995. *Health Promotion, Theory and Practice.* Basingstoke, UK: Macmillan.

Khouri, Gustavo, Maria Guadalupe Guzman, Luis Valdes, Isabel Carbonel, Delfina del Rosario, Susana Vázquez, José Laferte, Jorge Delgado and Maria V. Cabrera. 1998. Reemergence of dengue in Cuba: A 1997 epidemic in Santiago de Cuba. *Emerging Infectious Diseases* (4)1.

Labrador, Clarivel Presno, and Felix Sansó Soberat. 2004. 20 years of family medicine in Cuba. *MEDICC Review* 6(2). www.medicc.org/medicc_review/1104/pages/spotlight.html (accessed January 14, 2006).

Laurell, Asa Critina, and Olivia López Arellano. 1996. Market commodities and poor relief: The World Bank proposal for health. *International Journal of Health Services* 26:1–18.

Lemkau, Jeanne. 2004. Castro's clinic: In poor Havana the doctor makes house calls. *World View Magazine Online* 16 (4). www.worldviewmagazine.com/issues/article.cfm?id=125&issue=29 (accessed April 13, 2004).

London School of Economics. 2003. The Cuban Health System: its global impact and the lessons to be learned. www.lse.ac.uk/collections/pressAndInformation Office/newsAndEvents/archives/2003/Cuban_Health_System.htm (accessed June 4, 2003).

López Nistal, Libia Margarita, and Miriam Alicia Gran Álverez. 2005. La diabetes mellitus en Cuba. In *Temas De Estadística De Salud*. Dirección Nacional De Estadística. La Habana, Cuba: Ministério de Salud Pública de Cuba. www.dne.sld .cu/Libro/indexlibro.htm (accessed July 29, 2005).

MacDonald, Theodore H. 1985. *Making a New People: Education in Revolutionary Cuba*. Vancouver, BC: New Star Books.

———. 1999. *A Developmental Analysis of Cuba's Health Care System Since 1959*. Studies in Health and Human Services, 32. New York: Edwin Mallen.

———. 2001. *Third World Health Promotion and Its Dependence on First World Wealth*. Studies in Health and Human Services, 44. New York: Edwin Mallen.

Manderson, Lenore, and Linda M. Whiteford. 2000. Introduction. In *Global Policy/ Local Realities: The Fallacy of the Level Playing Field*. Boulder, Colo.: Lynne Rienner Press.

Martinez Almanza, Leocadio, Jesús Menéndez Jiménez, Elsy Cáceres Manso, Moisés Baly Baly, Enrique Vega Garcia, Osvaldo Prieto Ramos. 2000. The elderly in Cuba: main demographic trends, morbidity, and mortality. *MEDICC Review*, vol. II(1).

Más Lago, Pedro. 1995. Impacto social de la vacunación antipoliomielítica en Cuba. *Boletín del Ateneo Juan Cesar García* 3(1–2): 13–21.

MEDICC Review Staff. 2005. Profiles in commitment: conversations with ELAM students. *MEDICC Review* VII(8). www.medicc.org/medicc_review/0805/mr-features .html (accessed January 14, 2006).

Melville, Thomas, and Marjorie Melville. 1971. *Guatemala: The Politics of Land Ownership*. New York: Free Press.

Mesa-Lago, Carmelo. 1993. The social safety net in the two Cuban transitions. *Transition in Cuba: New Challenges for U.S. Policy*. Edited by Lisandro Pérez. Miami, Fla.: Cuban Research Institute, Florida International University.

———. 1998. Assessing economic and social performance in the Cuban transition of the 1990s. *World Development* 26(5): 857–76.

———. 2001. The Cuban economy in 1999–2001: Evaluation of performance and debate on the future. *Cuba in Transition*. Association for the Study of the Cuban Economy, 1–17.

———. 2005. Social and economic problems in Cuba during the crisis and subsequent recover. *CEPAL Review* 86, August 2005. 177–99.

———. 2006. Personal communication.

Morgan, Lynn M. 1990. International politics and primary health care in Costa Rica. *Social Science and Medicine* 30(2): 211–19.

———. 2001. Community participation in health: Perpetual allure, persistent challenge. *Health Policy and Planning* 16(3): 221–30.

Morsy, Soheir A. 1996. Political economy in medical anthropology. In *Handbook of Medical Anthropology: Contemporary Theory and Method*, edited by Carolyn Sargent and Thomas M. Johnson, rev. edition. Westport, Conn.: Greenwood Press.

Naciones Unidas (United Nations). 2002. *Anuario estadístico de América Latina y el Caribe 2001* (Statistical yearbook for Latin America and the Caribbean 2001). Santiago, Chile: Naciones Unidas, CEPAL/ECLAC.

Narayan, Deepa, et al. 2000. *Voices of the Poor: Crying Out for Change*. New York: Oxford University Press.

Nathanson, Constance A. 1996. Disease prevention as social change: Toward a theory of public health. *Population and Development Review* 22(4): 609–37.

National Center for Health Statistics. 1984. *Health, United States. 1984.* DHHS Pub. No. (PHS) 85–1232. Hyattsville, Md: National Center for Health Statistics.

———. 1998. *Health, United States, 1998 with Socioeconomic Status and Health Chartbook.* Hyattsville, Md.: U.S. Dept. of Health and Human Services, Centers for Disease Control and Prevention, National Center for Health Statistics.

———. 2002. *Health, United States, 2001 with Chartbook on Trends in the Health of Americans.* Hyattsville, Md.: U.S. Dept. of Health and Human Services, Centers for Disease Control and Prevention, National Center for Health Statistics.

Navarro, Vicente, and L. Shi. 2001. The political context for inequities and health. *International Journal of Health Services* 31:1–21.

Nayeri, Kamran. 1995. The Cuban health care system and factors currently undermining it. *Journal of Community Health* 20 (4): 321–34.

New York Times. 1998. Cuba to send doctors to Haiti. November 12. www.nytimes .com/aponline/i/AP-Haiti-Cuba.html (accessed June 30, 2005).

Novás, José Díaz, and José A. Fernández Socarrás. 1989. From municipal polyclinics to family doctor-and-nurse teams. *Revista Cubano de General Integral* 5(4): 556–64.

Nguyen, Vinh-Kim, and Karine Peschard. 2003. Anthropology, inequality, and disease. *Annual Review of Anthropology* 32:447–74.

Oficina Nacional de Estadísticas, Centro de Estudios de Población y Desarrollo. 1998.

Olivia Linares, José E., Lourdes E. Enríquez Sansevero, Rodolfo Cusa Serrano, Miguel Ángel Canetti Puebla, and José E. Fernández Britto Rodríguez. 2001. Enfermedad cerebrovascular: comportamiento en el Hospital Docente Dr. Salvador Allende durante 1997. *Revista Cubana De Investigaciones Biomédicas* 20 (3): 197–201.

Pan American Health Organization (PAHO). 1998. *Health in the Americas.* Scientific Publication no. 569. Washington, D.C: Pan American Health Organization.

———. 2002. In Travel Medicine program, PPHB, Health Canada. www.hc-sc.gc.ca/ pphb-dgspsp/tmp-pmv/2002/df0327_e.html (accessed June 30, 2002).

———. 2004. Basic country health profiles for the Americas: Cuba. www.paho.org/ English/DD/AIS/cp-192.htm (accessed 2005).

———. 2005. Basic country health profiles for the Americas: Cuba. www.paho.org/ English/DD/AIS/cp_192.htm (accessed July 29, 2005).

Parameswaran, Gowri. 2004. The Cuban response to the AIDS crisis: Human rights violation or just plain effective? *Dialectical Anthropology* 28 (3–4): 289–305.

Pardo, Candido López, Miguel Márquez, and Francisco Rojas Ochoa. 2005. Human development and equity in Latin American and the Caribbean. *MEDICC Review* vol. VII, no. 9, November/December.

Pérez, Jorge. 2002. An overview of the Cuban health system with an emphasis on the role of primary health care and immunization. In *Seminar on Cuban health system: Its evolution, accomplishments and challenges, December 11, 2001.* Edited by Lorena Barberia, Arachu Castro, and Dan Nemser, A9–A12. Cambridge, Mass.: David Rockefeller Center for Latin American Studies. www.medanthro.net/docs/ castro_cuba.pdf.

Pérez, Louis A. 1990. *Cuba and the United States: Ties of Singular Intimacy.* Athens: University of Georgia Press.

———. 1991. *Cuba Under the Platt Amendment 1902–1934,* Pittsburgh, Pa.: University of Pittsburgh Press.

———. 1995. *Cuba: Between Reform and Revolution*. 2nd ed. New York: Oxford University Press.

Pérez Caballero, Manuel Delfin, Lilliam Cordiés Jackson, Alfredo Vazquez Vigoa. 2000. Epidemiology of hypertension in Cuba. *MEDICC Review II*. www.medicc .org/Medicc?20Review//II/heart/html/epidemiology.html (accessed January 27, 2005).

Pérez-Stable, Marifeli 1994. *The Cuban Revolution: Origins, Course, and Legacy*. Oxford: Oxford University Press.

Prieto Ramos, Osvaldo, and Enrique Vega García. 1994. *Atención al Anciano en Cuba: Desarrollo y Perspectivas*. La Habana, Cuba: Ediciones Centro Iberoamericano para la Tercera Edad.

Putnam, Robert D. 2000. *Bowling Alone: The Collapse and Revival of American Community*. New York: Simon & Schuster.

Rathjens, George, and Jeffrey Boutwell. 2001. The Gates Award for global health, www.pugwash.org/reports/ees/ees8c.html (accessed June 28, 2005).

Reed, Gail A. 2001. Health News From Cuba. *MEDICC Review* III(1–2). www.medicc .org/Medicc%20Review/III/hiv-aids/news1.html (accessed July 14, 2005).

———. 2005. Where there were no doctors: First MDs graduate from Latin American medical school. *MEDICC Review* VII (8). www.medicc.org/medicc_review/0805/ top-story.html (accessed November 14, 2005).

Rifkin, Susan B. K., and Gill Walt. 1986. Why health improves: Defining the issues concerning "comprehensive primary health care" and "selective primary health care." *Social Science and Medicine* 23 (6): 559–66.

Ríos E., Tejeiros A. 1987. Evolución de la mortalidad en Cuba analizando un trienio de cada década del período revolucionario. Revista Cubana de Medicina General Integral. www.medicc.org/publications/medicc_review/II/heart/html/mortality .html.

Rojas Ochoa, Francisco. 2003. Situación, sistema y recursos humanos en salud para el desarrollo en Cuba. *Revista Cubana de Salud Público* 29(2): 157–69. http:// scieloprueba.sld.cu/scielo.php?script=sci_arttext&pid=S0864-34662003000200011 &lng=es&nrm=iso.

Sachs, Jeffrey D., and the Commission on Macroeconomics and Health. 2001. *Macroeconomics and Health: Investing in Health for Economic Development: Report.* Geneva: World Health Organization. www.un.org/esa/coordination/ecosoc/docs/ RT.K.MacroeconomicsHealth.pdf (accessed August 2, 2005).

Safa, Helen Icken, and Federación de Mujeres Cubanas. 1989. *Women, Industrialization and State Policy in Cuba*. Working Paper #133. University of Notre Dame, Ind.: Kellogg Institute. www.nd.edu/~kellogg/WPS/133.pdf.

Santana, Sarah. 1987. The Cuban health care system: Responsiveness to changing population needs and demands. *World Development* 15 (1):113–25.

Santiago Luis, Ricardo, and Silvia Haydée Delgado Zapata. 2000. Editorial: Enfermedades cerebrovasculares. Reto de la Salud Pública Cubana en el presente quinquenio. *Resumed* 13 (4): 139–41.

Scheper-Hughes, Nancy. 1993. AIDS, public policy, and human rights in Cuba. *Lancet* 342 (8877): 965–67.

Showstack, Jonathan, Arlyss Anderson Rothman, and Sue Hasmiller, eds. 2004. *The Future of Primary Care*. New York: Jossey-Bass.

Surgeon General's Advisory Committee on Smoking and Health. 1964. *Smoking and Health: Report of the Advisory Committee to the Surgeon General of the Public Health Service*. Washington, D.C.: U.S. Dept. of Health, Education, and Welfare, Public Health Service. www.cdc.gov/tobacco/sgr/sgr%5F1964/sgr64.htm.

Susman, Ed. 2003. U.S. could learn from Cuban AIDS policy. *AIDS* 17(3):N7–N8.

Szreter, Simon. 1988. The importance of social intervention in Britain's mortality decline. *Social History of Medicine* 1 (1): 1–38.

———. 1997. Economic growth, disruption, deprivation, disease, and death: On the importance of the politics of public health for development. *Population and Development Review* 23 (4): 693–728.

Torres, C.A. 1993. "From the 'Pedagogy of the Oppressed' to 'A Luta Continua': The political pedagogy of Paulo Freire" in P. McLarend and P. Lenard. eds., *Freire: A Critical Encounter*. London: Routledge.

Townsend, Peter, and N. Davidson. 1992. *Inequities in Health*. London: Penguin.

Trumbull, Charles. 2001. Prostitution and sex tourism in Cuba. *Cuba in Transition: Papers and Proceedings of the Eleventh Annual Meeting of the Association for the Study of the Cuban Economy (ASCE), Miami, FL, August 3–5, 2002*, 356–71. Miami, Fla.: Association for the Study of the Cuban Economy. http://lanic.utexas.edu/project/asce/pdfs/volume11/trumbull2.pdf (accessed August 2, 2005).

Turshen, Meredith. 1999. *Privatizing Health Services in Africa*. New Brunswick, N.J.: Rutgers Press.

UN Millennium Project. 2005. *Investing in Development: a Practical Plan to Achieve the Millennium Development Goals*. New York: Millennium Project Secretariat. www.unmillenniumproject.org/goals/ (accessed December 31, 2005).

UNICEF. 2005. At a glance: Cuba: Statistics. www.unicef.org/infobycountry/cuba_statistics.html (accessed July 29, 2005).

United Kingdom National Statistics. www.statistics.gov.uk/cci/nuggest.asp?id=861 (accessed March 8, 2005).

United Nations, Department of Economic and Social Affairs, Population Division. 2002. *World Population Ageing, 1950–2050*. New York: United Nations.

United Nations Population and Development (UNPD) 1999. *Investigación sobre desarrollo humano y equidad en Cuba*. Centro de Investigaciones de la Economía Mundial. hdr.undp.org/docs/reports/national/CUB_Cuba/Cuba_199-_sp.pdf (Last accessed October 12, 2007).

United Nations Statistics Division. 2005. *Demographic and Social Statistics*. http://unstats.un.org/unsd/demographic/default.htm (accessed July 29, 2005).

U.S. Department of Health and Human Services (USDHHS). 2001. *Health, United States, 2001: Socioeconomic Status and Health Chartbook*. Hyattsville, Md.: U.S. Dept. of Health and Human Services, Centers for Disease Control and Prevention, National Center for Health Statistics.

———. 2002. *U.S. National Vital Statistics Report* 50, no. 16 (September 16, 2002). Hyattsville, Md.: U.S. Dept. of Health and Human Services, Centers for Disease Control and Prevention, National Center for Health Statistics.

U.S. Department of State. 2005. Background note: Cuba. www.state.gov/r/pa/ei/bgn/2886.htm (accessed June 30, 2005).

Valdes, Nelson P. 2001. Health in Cuba (pre 1959–1982). www.unm.edu/~nvaldes/Cuba/health.htm (accessed August 2, 2005).

Vega Garcia, E. 2000. Personal communication.

Victoria, Irene Perdomo, María Luisa Torres Páez, and María E. Astraín Rodríguez. 1999. Morbilidad y mortalidad de los ancianos en el municipio Habana Vieja (1994–1996). *Revista Cubana Salud Pública* 25 (2): 143–53.

Wagstaff, Adam. 2002. Poverty and health sector inequalities. *Bull World Health Organ* 80 (2): 97–105.

Waitzkin, Howard, and Theron Britt. 1989. Changing the structure of medical discourse: Implications of cross-national comparisons. *Journal of Health and Social Behavior* 30:436–49.

Waitzkin, Howard, Karen Wald, Ross Danielson, and Lisa Robinson. 1997. Primary care in Cuba: Low- and high-technology developments pertinent to family medicine. *Journal of Family Practice* 45 (3): 250–58.

Walsh, J. A., and K. S. Warren. 1979. Selective primary health care: An interim strategy for disease control in developing countries. *New England Journal of Medicine* 301 (18): 967–74.

Warman, Andrea. 2001. Living the Revolution: Cuban health workers. *Journal of Clinical Nursing* 10:311–19.

Warren, K. S. 1988. The evolution of selective primary health care. *Social Science and Medicine* 26 (9): 891–98.

Wayland, Coral, and Jerome Crowder. 2002. Disparate views of community in primary health care: Understanding how perceptions influence success. *Medical Anthropology Quarterly* 16 (2): 230–47.

Whiteford, Linda. 1990. A question of adequacy: Primary health care in the Dominican Republic. *Social Science and Medicine* 30 (2): 221–26.

———. 1993. International economic policies and child health. *Social Science and Medicine* 37 (11): 1391–1400.

———. 1996. Political economy, gender and the social production of health and illness. In *Gender and Health: An International Perspective*, edited by Carolyn Sargent and Caroline Brettell, 242–59. Upper Saddle River, N.J.: Prentice Hall.

———. 1997. The ethnoecology of dengue fever. *Medical Anthropology Quarterly* 11 (2): 202–23.

———. 1998a. Sembrando el futuro: globalization and the commodification of health. In *Crossing Currents: Continuity and Change in Latin America*. edited by Michael B. Whiteford and Scott Whiteford, 264–70. Upper Saddle River, N.J.: Prentice Hall.

———. 1998b. Children's health as accumulated capital: Structural adjustment in the Dominican Republic and Cuba. In *Small Wars: The Cultural Politics of Childhood*, edited by Nancy Scheper-Hughes and Carolyn Sargent, 186–203. Berkeley: University of California Press.

———. 2000. Idioms of hope and despair: Local identity, globalization and health in Cuba and the Dominican Republic. In *Global Health Policy/Local Realities: The Fallacy of the Level Playing Field*. Edited by Linda M. Whiteford and Lenore Manderson, 57–78. Boulder, Colo.: Lynne Rienner Press.

———. 2005. Casualties In The Globalization Of Water: A Moral Economy Of Perspective. In *Globalization, Water and Health: Resources in Times of Scarcity*. Edited by Linda M. Whiteford and Scott Whiteford, 25–45. Santa Fe, N.M.: School of American Research Press.

Whiteford, Linda M., and Linda Bennett. 2005. Applied anthropology and health and medicine. In *Applied Anthropology: Domains of Application*, edited by Satish Kedia and John van Willigen. Westport, Conn.: Praeger Publishers.

Whiteford, Linda M., and Jeannine Coreil. 1997. The household ecology of disease transmission: Dengue fever in the Dominican Republic. In *Anthropology and Infectious Disease*, edited by Peter Brown and Marsha Inhorn, 145–73. Australia: Gordon and Breach Publishers.

Whiteford, Linda M., and Beverly Hill. 2005. The political economy of dengue in Cuba and the Dominican Republic. In *Globalization, Health, and the Environment*, edited by Greg Guest. Lanham, Md.: AltaMira Press.

Whiteford, Linda, and Lois LaCivita Nixon. 1999. Comparative health systems: Emerging convergences and globalization. In *The Handbook of Social Studies in Health and Medicine*, edited by Gary L. Albrecht, Ray Fitzpatrick, and Susan Scrimshaw, 440–53. London: Sage Publications.

Whiteford, Linda, and Lenore Manderson. 2000. *Global Policy/Local Realities: The Fallacy of the Level Playing Field*. Boulder, Colo.: Lynne Rienner Press.

Whiteford, Linda, and Scott Whiteford. 2005a. Concluding comments: Future challenges. In *Globalization, Water and Health: Resources in Times of Scarcity*, edited by Linda M. Whiteford and Scott Whiteford, 255–67. Santa Fe, N.M.: School of American Research Press.

———. 2005b. Paradigm change. In *Globalization, Water and Health: Resources in Times of Scarcity*, edited by Linda M. Whiteford and Scott Whiteford, 3–17. Santa Fe, N.M.: School of American Research Press.

———, eds. 2005c. *Globalization, Water and Health: Resources in Times of Scarcity*. Santa Fe, N.M.: School of American Research Press.

Whiteford, Scott, and Scott Witter. 1999. Water insecurity and infectious diseases. *International Review of Comparative Public Policy* 11:63–82.

Whitehead, M. 1992. The health divide. In P. Townsend and N. Davidson, eds., *Inequities in Health*. London: Penguin.

Whitehead, Margaret, Göran Dahlgren, and Timothy Evans. 2001. Equity and health sector reforms: Can low-income countries escape the medical poverty trap? *Lancet* 358 (9284): 833–36.

Wilkerson, Richard G. 1992. National mortality rates: The impact of inequality? *American Journal of Public Health* 82 (8):1082–84.

———. 1996. *Unhealthy Societies: The Afflictions of Inequality*. London: Routledge.

Wilkerson, Richard G. and Michael Marmot, eds. 2003. *Social Determinants of Health: the Solid Facts*. Copenhagen: World Health Organization, Regional Office for Europe.

———. 1998. *Social Determinants of Health: The Solid Facts*. Copenhagen: Centre for Urban Health, World Health Organization, Regional Office for Europe.

World Bank. 1993. *Investing in Health: World Development Report*. New York: Oxford University Press for the World Bank.

———. 2001. *World Development Report 2000/2001*. New York: Oxford University Press.

World Health Organization (WHO). 1978. *The Declaration of Alma-Ata: Primary Health Care is the Key to Health for All*. Geneva: World Health Organization/ UNICEF.

———. 2000. *World Health Report 2000.* Geneva: World Health Organization.

———. 2001. *Investing in Health: A Summary of the Findings of the Commission on Macroeconomics and Health.* Geneva: World Health Organization.

———. 2003a. Global Meeting on Future Strategic Directions for Primary Health Care, October 27–29. www.who.int/chronic_conditions/primary_health_care/en/ (accessed December 27, 2004).

———. 2003b. *WHO Mortality Database.* Geneva: World Health Organization.

———. 2003c. *A Global Review of Primary Health Care: Emerging Messages. Non-Communicable Diseases and Mental Health, Evidence for Information and Policy.* Geneva: World Health Organization.

———. 2004. Cuba, all cancers. http://www-dep.iarc.fr/ and http://www.who.int/whosis/ (accessed July 29, 2005).

———. 2006. *What is the Evidence of Effectiveness of Empowerment to Improve Health?* Copenhagen: World Health Organization

Wright, R.A. Community-oriented primary care: The cornerstone of health care reform, *Journal of the American Medical Association,* 1993; 269 (19): 2544–47.

Zipperer, M. 2005. HIV/AIDS prevention and control: The Cuban response. *Lancet Infectious Diseases* 5 (7): 400. http://infection.thelancet.com (accessed August 26, 2005).

Index

About the Authors

Linda M. Whiteford is professor of medical anthropology at the University of South Florida and has served as president of the Society of Applied Anthropology. In addition to her work on Cuba, she has conducted research in the Dominican Republic, Ecuador, Bolivia, Nicaragua, Guatemala, and Mexico, and has received research funding from the National Science Foundation and the Global Center for Disaster Management and Humanitarian Assistance. Dr. Whiteford has also served as a consultant to the United States Agency for International Development, the World Bank, and the Pan American Health Organization. She was the Visiting Scholar of the Year at Santa Clara University, and the recipient of the Foster Distinguished Lecture Award at Southern Methodist University and the President's Award for Scholarly Excellence at the University of South Florida. She is the author of numerous publications, including "The Political Economy of Dengue in Cuba and the Dominican Republic" (with Beverly Hill) in *Globalization, Health, and the Environment* (2005); "Applied Anthropology and Health and Medicine" (with Linda Bennett) in *Applied Anthropology: Domains of Application* (S. Kedia and J. van Willigen, eds., 2005); and "Casualties in the Globalization of Water: A Moral Economy of Perspective" in *Globalization, Water and Health: Resources in Times of Scarcity* (L. M. Whiteford and S. Whiteford, eds., 2005).

Laurence G. Branch is professor of health policy and management at the College of Public Health at the University of South Florida and holds a joint appointment as professor in the Department of Internal Medicine in the College of Medicine and a courtesy appointment as professor at the Florida Mental Health Institute. He previously was dean of the College of Public

Health at the University of South Florida. Before that he was a research professor in Duke University's Center for the Study of Aging and Human Development (1995–2002) and was the director of Duke's medical doctor/master's in public health program and director of its long-term care research program. He has also held faculty appointments from Harvard Medical School and Harvard School of Public Health from 1978 to 1986 and from Boston University School of Medicine from 1986 to 1996. He contributes regularly to the health policy field as evidenced by over 150 articles in peer-reviewed journals, more than 50 book chapters and monographs, and two edited books. One of his previous articles on Cuba is entitled "An Introduction to the Cuban Health Care System: The Case of Elder Care," coauthored with Evelinn Borrayo, James Sykes, and Enrique Vega and published in *Global Ageing* (2004).

William M. Anderson Library
West Shore Community Col
3000 N. Stiles Road
Scottville, MI 49454
231-843-5529
library@westshore.edu

22046588R00084

Made in the USA
San Bernardino, CA
08 January 2019